Classic Warplanes

BOEING
B-17
FLYING
FORTRESS

Doug Richardson

GALLERY BOOKS

An Imprint of W. H. Smith Publishers Inc.
112 Madison Avenue
New York City 10016

A SALAMANDER BOOK

©Salamander Books Ltd. 1991
129-137 York Way,
London N7 9LG,
United Kingdom.

ISBN 0-8317-1406-9

This edition published in 1991 by Gallery
Books, an imprint of W.H. Smith
Publishers, Inc., 112 Madison Avenue,
New York, New York 10016.

Gallery Books are available for bulk
purchase for sales promotions and
premium use. For details, write or
telephone the Manager of Special Sales,
W.H. Smith Publishers, Inc., 112
Madison Avenue, New York, New York
10016. (212) 532-660.

All correspondence concerning the
content of this volume should be
addressed to Salamander Books Ltd.

This book may not be sold outside the
United States of America or Canada.

CREDITS

Editor: Bob Munro
Designers: Oxprint Ltd., England
Color Artwork: ©Pilot Press, England
Three-view, side-view and cutaway
drawings: ©Pilot Press, England
Filmset by: The Old Mill, England
Color separation by Graham Curtis
Repro, England
Printed in Belgium by Proost International
Book Production, Turnhout

AUTHOR

DOUG RICHARDSON is a defense journalist and author specializing in
the fields of aviation, guided missiles and electronics. After a successful career
as an electronics and aerospace engineer he moved into journalism. He has been
the Defense Editor of "Flight International", Editor of "Military Technology",
and Editor of "Defense Materiel" before becoming a full-time freelance writer.

He has written many Salamander books including "The Illustrated Guide to
Electronic Warfare", "The F-16 Fact File", "The AH-1 Fact File", "An Illustrated
Survey of the West's Modern Fighters" and "Stealth Warplanes".

CONTENTS

TODAY, the name of Boeing is synonymous with the production of civil airliners, examples of which flow off the company's production line day after day, year after year. Times are good for Boeing: its products are in demand; its order books are full for years to come. Yet times have not always been so good for one of the oldest and most famous aircraft manufacturing companies in the United States of America.

As the 1920s gave way to the 1930s, Boeing was struggling to survive. The First World War — the ''War to end all Wars'' — was long settled, and military requirements and orders had been drastically curtailed. To make matters worse, Boeing found itself fighting an economic war, as the company struggled to survive the ravages of the Great Depression.

The company's saviour came in the form of a new, all-metal, monoplane airliner, known in-house as the Boeing Model 247. This revolutionary aircraft made its debut in 1932, and United Air Lines immediately placed an order for no less than 60 examples. The sale provided Boeing with desperately needed revenue, and the company soon put it to good use to finance the development of another new and equally revolutionary aircraft design. But the new aircraft was not an airliner. It was a bomber.

In 1933 the United States Army Air Corps (USAAC) began to consider its future bomber requirements; but rather than following the traditional route of specifying a set of needs which contemporary aerospace technology and manufacturing processes could comfortably accommodate, the USAAC, in a bold and far-sighted move, tried to envisage what it might need in the future.

Studies were conducted of design concepts with wing spans three to four times that of the twin-engined Martin B-10 then in front-line service.

Below: Signalling a new age in the field of airliner design, Boeing's Model 247 provided the company with much-needed revenue, some of which funded the Model 299.

Above: While the USAAC looked to the future, the ungainly and underpowered Martin B-10 held its own in the front line. But in truth, its days were numbered.

Maximum weights ten to 20 times greater than that of the Martin bomber were also considered.

These tests led in the autumn of 1933 to a specification for what was known as "Project A": a Very Long Range Bomber with a wing span in the region of 150ft (45.75m); a maximum weight of approximately 60,000lb (27,240kg); a range in the region of 5,000 miles (8,045km); and a bombload of 2,000lb (908kg). These were demanding requirements indeed, but a design contract was formally issued to Boeing on 28 June 1934 for the construction of one aircraft.

Known to Boeing as the Model 294, but given the military designation XB-15, the new aircraft was always seen as a technology demonstrator rather than a prototype for the next USAAC bomber. Just what the USAAC had in mind to replace its fleet of B-10s became apparent on 8 August 1934, when Circular 35-26 was formally issued.

Right: The XB-15's truly massive dimensions are apparent in this view of the airborne Goliath as it dwarfs another Boeing product, the P-26 Peashooter fighter.

The new bomber was to have a maximum speed of at least 200mph (322km/h) while operating at 10,000ft (3,050m), although ideally it should be able to reach 250mph (402km/h) at the same ceiling. A cruising speed of 170mph to 220mph (273.5km/h to 353km/h) was required, as was a service ceiling of 20,000ft to 25,000ft (6,100m to 7,625m) and a maximum range of 1,020 miles (1,641km), although the USAAC hoped for this latter figure to be increased to 2,200 miles (3,540km). The aircraft was to be "multi-engined" (a term then used to denote the use of two engines), and a crew of between four and six was envisaged. Designs had to be company-funded, and were to be submitted to the USAAC for testing in a year's time. In modern parlance, it was a "winner takes all" competition, with bids requested for a production run of up to 220 aircraft.

TAKING SHAPE

Boeing started work on what would become the Model 299 on 18 June 1934, and began to cut metal on 16 August. Building a prototype would take most of the company's manpower, and consume most of its capital. Consequently, on 26 September 1934, the board assigned $275,000 for the project. The aircraft created by a team of 73 engineers was a mid-wing monoplane about two-thirds the size of the XB-15: 68ft (20.74m) long, with a 103ft (31.41m) wing span, it would be powered by four 750hp Pratt & Whitney R-1690-E Hornet single-row, seven-cylinder, air-cooled radial engines. Wind tunnel tests suggested a top speed of at least 235mph (378km/h), and a maximum range of 3,000 miles (4,827km).

Just as Boeing's earlier Model 215 bomber had used technology from the civil Model 200 Monomail, so the new bomber was able to draw on the Model 247, which had flown for the first time on 8 February, 1933.

Meeting The Need

The Model 299 would have an all-metal wing similar to that planned for the XB-15 but scaled down in size and with tubular truss spars, between which were four metal tanks with a total capacity of 1,700 US gal (6,434.5 litres) of fuel. The cowled engines would be fronted by constant-speed propellers with controllable pitch, and the undercarriage would retract into the inboard nacelles. Design of the fuselage drew on that of the Model 247, but incorporated dorsal, ventral and lateral blister transparencies for .30in or .50in (7.62mm or 12.7mm) calibre machine-guns, plus an internal weapons bay fitted with electrically-operated bomb doors. Normal crew would consist of a pilot, co-pilot, bombardier, navigator/radio operator, and a total of four gunners.

Construction started in late-1934, and the board later allocated a further $150,000 needed to complete the job. Progress with the new Model 299 soon eclipsed that on the larger "Project A". In June 1935, the latter was given the official military designation XB-15; but at a time when the Model 299 was rapidly taking shape, the larger aircraft had barely gotten to the stage of engine selection.

Below: What was supposed to be another routine test flight from Wright Field on 30 October 1935, ended in disaster when the Model 299 crashed just after take-off.

Bearing the civil registration X13372, the Model 299 was rolled out of the Boeing factory at Seattle, Washington, on 17 July 1935. A newspaper reporter who watched the event nicknamed the impressive aircraft the "Flying Fortress". The aircraft took to the air for the first time early on the morning of 28 July. Just twelve days later, she was ready for delivery to the USAAC. Test programmes were short in those days!

Early on the morning of 10 August a Boeing crew set out on the delivery flight from Seattle to Wright Field, located just outside Dayton, Ohio. The 2,100-mile (3,379km) flight took just over nine hours, with the Model 299 achieving an enviable average speed of 233mph (375km/h).

Two rival, twin-engined designs were also under evaluation: Martin's B-12 was a modified version of the

Above: With the American media present in force, the sleek and imposing Model 299 basks in the limelight following its public debut at the Boeing plant.

tried and tested B-10, while Douglas had based its DB-1 on its DC-2 commercial airliner. At first it seemed that the Boeing aircraft was a certain winner, as its four engines gave it a clear and valuable edge in performance over the Douglas and Martin designs.

DISASTER STRIKES

But on the morning of 30 October 1935, tragedy struck. The Model 299 stalled immediately after take-off, and crashed close to the Wright Field runway. Rescuers were able to get to the pilots, while two other crewmen scrambled out from the rear of the aircraft. Almost immediately, investigators realized what had happened. The aircraft had been fitted with locks intended to prevent wind from moving the control surfaces when the aircraft was parked. On the final flight, the crew had simply forgotten to release these locks. USAAC test pilot Major Ployer Hill died in hospital that afternoon, Boeing chief test pilot Les Tower soon afterwards.

As a result of the crash, Boeing was effectively disqualified from the final

Above: With the loss of the sole Model 299, the USAAC was forced to choose the Douglas DB-1 as its competition winner. In military service, it became the B-18 Bolo.

stage of testing — evaluation flights by service aircrew — and the USAAC subsequently ordered the Douglas aircraft into production as the B-18 Bolo. Despite the crash, the USAAC had been sufficiently impressed by the Model 299 to order a batch of thirteen examples plus a structural test airframe. A contract for these aircraft, officially designated YB-17s, was subsequently awarded to Boeing on 12 January 1936.

During its short career, the Model 299 had shown areas for potential improvement, so modifications were made to the design. The most obvious new feature of the YB-17 (later redesignated Y1B-17) was the change from the original dual-oleo main landing gear to a new single-oleo pattern which would make wheel and tyre changes much easier. The engines were also changed in favour of the 850hp Wright R-1820-39 Cyclone.

Fabric-covered flaps replaced the original metal units, while other detailed changes improved areas such as the fuel and oxygen systems, instrumentation, and de-icing arrangements.

LOSS AND GAIN

Testing of the Y1B-17 in flight revealed that the engines and brakes were prone to overheating — a combination of the two problems led to the loss of the first Y1B-17 during its third flight. On landing after the flight had been cut short due to engine problems, the aircraft nosed over on touchdown. No-one was injured, and an investigation showed that the brakes had jammed as a result of being retracted in an overheated condition after take-off.

On 3 August 1937, the USAAC ordered 10 production B-17s with uprated engines for greater speed and height. Other changes introduced by this new version (designated the B-17B) included a larger rudder, redesigned nose, and a modified fuel system. On the earlier aircraft, the entire nose bubble was able to rotate around the aircraft's axis, allowing the single .50in (12.7mm) machine-gun to cover targets approaching from any direction. This proved to be none too successful, so the definitive design which replaced it

comprised a fixed pattern made up of several sections of Plexiglas, with a ball-and-socket machine-gun mount in the upper starboard section.

The lower front section of the nose consisted of a flat panel through which the bomb-aimer could sight his targets. The small aiming window used on the Y1B-17 was deleted, and the bomb-aimer's position moved forward to the extreme nose. On the Y1B-17, this individual had also acted as navigator, but now the two roles would be performed by separate crewmen. The Direction-Finding (DF) loop antenna formerly mounted above the cockpit was also moved to a new location under the nose.

Twelve of the 13 Y1B-17s were issued to the 2nd Bomb Group (BG), which became the Army's only four-engined bomber unit. In 1938, this unit won the *MacKay* Trophy for a formation flight from Langley Field, Virginia, to South America; but not all of the 2nd BG's exploits were received too favourably. In May 1938, three of the unit's aircraft flew a highly-publicized

Below: Despite selection of the Douglas design, the USAAC lost no time in ordering a small batch of Model 299s, to be known as YB-17s in military service.

practice intercept sortie of the Italian liner *Rex*. The immediate result was a US Navy-instigated ban on future long-range airborne maritime sorties!

The need for a structural-test airframe was eliminated when a Y1B-17 was exposed to freak stresses during a

Below: The revised nose glazing of the B-17B/C is evident on this C-model assigned to the Army's Air Development Center. Note also the highly polished metal finish.

thunderstorm encountered on a test flight. This had subjected the airframe to stresses greater than those planned for the ground-based structural testing specimen, so the airframe was completed as a 14th aircraft and designated Y1B-17A, and equipped as a turbo-supercharger test-bed.

First flight of the Y1B-17A took place on 20 November 1938. At first, the turbo-superchargers released their exhaust from the top of the engine nacelles, but this had a bad effect on

the flow of air across the wing upper surface, causing severe buffeting. The installation was redesigned so that the turbo-supercharger and its exhaust could be moved to the lower part of the engine nacelle.

RECORD BREAKER

The superchargers boosted service ceiling from 31,000ft (9,455m) to 38,000ft (11,590m), while the top speed was raised from 239mph (385km/h) at 5,000ft (1,525m) to 271mph (436km/h) at 25,000ft (7,625m). The aircraft was used to set a load/speed record over a distance of 621 miles (1,000km), as well as setting a load/altitude record. This work on turbo-supercharging had been entirely funded by Boeing, and it led to a USAAC order that all future B-17s (including the B-17B) be fitted with these systems.

At the end of March 1940, Boeing delivered the 39th and final B-17B. None would see combat, but the final example was not retired until January 1946. As the ''Phoney War'' dragged on, with the Allies awaiting the inevitable German attack toward the West, the USAAC looked at ways of improving the B-17. Boeing was already working on the B-17C, which would carry .50in (12.7mm) machine-guns in all positions but the nose, where the lighter .30in (7.62mm) weapons were to be retained.

Above: With war looming on the horizon, the natural metal finish prevelant on early B-17s began to give way to a more subdued set of camouflage colours, as evident on this B-17D of the 19th BG.

Right: Formating nicely with the camera-ship, this Flying Fortress has had its camouflage extended at the expense of its colourful and distinctive red, white and blue rudder striping.

This change in armament removed the blister gun positions used on earlier B-17s. The waist blisters were replaced by pedestal-mounted guns firing through teardrop-shaped windows, while the top blister was replaced by a sliding Plexiglas fairing, and the ventral blister was replaced by a more solid "bathtub" structure. Extra sockets for the machine-guns were added in the nose, while a teardrop-shaped antenna replaced the DF loop mounted under the nose.

Combat survivability was a key issue, with the USAAC already demanding further improvements such as armour-plating of vital areas of the aircraft, and yet more guns, particularly to defend the tail area. On 11 May 1940, studies of improved armament were submitted to the USAAC, which decided that future B-17s would be fitted with power-operated turrets above and below the fuselage, plus twin guns in the tail and radio operator's positions. The heavier .50in (12.7mm) guns would be fitted

in all positions except the nose, while the waist gunners' teardrop windows would be replaced by large rectangular glazed panels. Ability to absorb combat damage would be improved by the installation of extensive armour-plating and self-sealing fuel tanks.

Some of these changes were already featured in the B-17C and planned for the B-17D, but the B-17E would be the first truly combat-ready model. While Boeing worked flat out to develop the E-model, the production line was kept busy with the earlier models. Only 38 B-17Cs were built, comprising 18 for the USAAC and 20 for the first export customer, namely the United Kingdom's Royal Air Force (RAF).

Production of the B-17C had ended by November 1940, and the next 42 aircraft were sufficiently different to justify the designation B-17D. The upper and lower gun positions were modified to accept twin .50in (12.7mm) machine-guns, while internal changes included the installation of self-sealing fuel tanks and more ar-

mour plating. In addition, cowl flaps were added to the engine nacelles. Other modifications included redesigned bomb racks and bomb release mechanism, a low-pressure oxygen system, and a change from 12 to 24-volt electrics. Deliveries of the B-17D started in February 1941, with the last examples being completed by the end of April.

FROM D TO E

A smooth transition to the B-17E had been planned. No prototype was built; the first example would be the first production aircraft. In theory, this should have followed right after the final B-17D, with the line delivering B-17Es from April 1941 onwards; but

Below: All lined up and ready to go, these factory-fresh B-17Cs formed part of an order for 20 such machines for the United Kingdom. In RAF service, they were known as Fortress Is.

shortage of material and trained man-power made this impossible. At one point in the winter of 1940/41, material shortages had even forced Boeing to lay off workers and shut down part of the assembly line!

By the spring of 1941, the US faced the growing realization that it would become involved in the war against Germany; and in April, an ''Army Special Observer Group'' headed by Major-General James E. Chaney was established in London to begin preliminary work on setting up a UK-based heavy bomber force.

His arrival was well-timed, for the RAF had just received its first B-17Cs. Known as Fortress Is, these were to be issued to No. 90 Squadron, based at RAF West Raynham, Norfolk. In May, the new squadron started operations. Meanwhile, the USAAC was preparing to deploy the new D-model,

Below: A Fortress I assigned to No. 90 Squadron, RAF, roars off at the start of another mission. On 8 July 1941, the unit blooded the B-17 in combat over Europe when it bombed Wilhelmshaven.

sending 21 examples to Hickam Field, Hawaii, to join the 5th BG(H).

By mid-1941, the RAF was ready to try the Fortress I in combat; and on 8 July, two such aircraft bombed Wilhelmshaven in Germany from an altitude of 30,000ft (9,150m). It was an inauspicious beginning. The bombs missed their target, and the guns froze at altitude, but the two aircraft made it safely back to base. On 24 July, RAF Fortress Is attacked the German battleship *Gneisenau.* Hits were claimed, no bombers were lost, but once more the guns froze.

By September, the RAF had mounted 26 daylight raids against targets such as Emden, Kiel, Brest, Bremen, Rotterdam, Borkum and Wilhelmshaven for the loss of eight Fortress Is, some in crash landings. Reliability had been poor, with 26 of the planned 51 sorties being aborted for one reason or another.

RAF experience suggested that the Flying Fortress was far from combat ready. The Norden bombsight was not living up to expectations; the defensive armament was inadequate — particularly towards the rear; the guns

tended to freeze at altitude; and the aircraft was vulnerable to enemy gun-fire, and tended to burn when hit. RAF crews also complained of icing problems, oxygen system failures, and other mechanical problems.

By operating the aircraft in small numbers, the British had ignored the basic US concept that Flying Fortresses should fly in large formations, protected by their mutual firepower. Even so, it was clear that in its current form, the aircraft was not suitable for combat missions over Europe. The RAF promptly reassigned its Fortress Is to the Middle East. Aware that the RAF experience had shown unexpected problems in flying at altitudes of up to 30,000ft (9,150m), Boeing started a programme of high-altitude testing using the B-17C.

TENSION MOUNTS

On 5 September 1941, the first B-17E finally took to the air, 150 days behind schedule. As diplomatic relations between the USA and Japan deteriorated in the autumn of 1941, more B-17s were moved to bases in the

Above: While a newly-built B-17E awaits a final ground inspection, one of its compatriots takes off from the Boeing plant at Seattle on its delivery flight.

Above: Easily distinguishable from earlier models by virtue of its greatly enlarged and reconfigured vertical tail surfaces, the B-17E was also more heavily armed.

Pacific. In early September, nine B-17Ds from Hickam Field, Hawaii, flew to Clark Field in the Philippines, joining the 19th BG(H) of the recently retitled United States Army Air Force (USAAF). In October, Boeing delivered 12 more B-17s; and on 16 October, a force of 26 aircraft — a mixture of B-17Ds and some updated B-17Cs — arrived at Hickam Field, bringing the 19th BG(H) force up to operational strength.

The tempo of deliveries speeded up. In November, Boeing delivered 25 B-17Es, and was due to deliver a further 35 in the following month. That plan was rudely interrupted.

The Japanese attack on Pearl Har-

bor on the morning of 7 December 1941 caught Hickam Field's 12 B-17s on the ground. Most were destroyed. While the attack was still under way, twelve unarmed B-17Ds from the 7th BG arrived over Hickam. One was destroyed just after it landed; the remainder were damaged either by Japanese fighters or anti-aircraft (AA)

fire from "friendly" ground forces.

Later that same day, Boeing executive Jake Harman made a phone call to Plant Two at Seattle. The conversation was concise and to the point:

"Start building airplanes."

"How many?"

"My instructions are just start building. Never mind the schedules. Tell us how much money and what things you need, when."

In the hands of USAAF pilots, the Boeing B-17 Flying Fortress was well and truly at war.

Right: The delivery of as many B-17Es as quickly as possible became a top priority after the mauling received by US Pacific forces in December 1941.

THE effect of the Japanese air strikes on 7 December 1941 against the USAAF's B-17 force based in the Pacific region was as devastating as that mounted against the US Navy's battleships anchored in Pearl Harbor. Three hours after the attack began, most of the twelve B-17s caught on the ramp at Hickam Field had been destroyed. Of the dozen unarmed B-17Ds that arrived over Hickam at just the wrong time, eleven were damaged and one destroyed.

Nine hours later, the Japanese turned their attention to targets in the Philippine Islands, including Clark Field, home to the 19th BG(H) and its B-17s. Once again, the aircraft were caught on the ground, and 18 were destroyed. Luckily, the 14th BS(H) had been detached to Del Monte, a small airfield on the island of Mindanao some 600 miles (965km) to the south, and so escaped destruction. Nevertheless, the Japanese attacks had ravaged the USAAF's B-17 force.

On 9 December, the B-17s at Del Monte began flying a series of reconnaissance missions, searching the seas for the Japanese invasion force. The next day, a Japanese convoy was sighted off the coast of Luzon, and five 19th BG(H) aircraft took off to attack it. Several hits were reported, but none of the vessels was sunk. However, the engagement was a historic one in that it marked the first instance of bombs being dropped from aircraft in US service during the Second World War.

A second attack on the convoy made use of several B-17s now back at Clark Field. One of them, a B-17C flown by Captain Colin Kelly, attacked what it reported as a battleship, scoring several hits in the process. Heading home to Clark Field, the lumbering bomber

Above: Working flat out to meet urgent orders for just over 500 B-17Es, the Boeing production line at Seattle was a hive of activity when this photograph was taken in January 1942.

was intercepted and attacked by several Mitsubishi A6M Zero fighters. Badly damaged and on fire, the B-17C managed to get back to base, where the crew bailed out. Sadly, the aircraft blew up before Kelly could jump clear. The US Navy later claimed the sinking of the battleship *Haruna*, but Japanese records show no ships of any kind lost that day.

Whatever the explanation of the incident, it served to confirm what the RAF had experienced during its early daylight bombing raids with its Fortress Is. The B-17, the so-called Flying Fortress, was highly vulnerable to enemy fire. Soon, the remaining early-model B-17s were being flown back to the United States, there to be used in secondary roles such as training. In their place would come the B-17E, the first truly battleworthy version of the Boeing bomber.

In production and available for combat when the United States found itself fully involved in the Second World War, the B-17E's fuselage was 73ft 1½in (22.30m) long, and made up of four main assemblies which were bolted together. Longitudinal stringers, plus vertical bulkheads located at various points down the length of the fuselage, provided added strength.

Just aft of the glazed nose was a forward-facing seat for the bombardier. Immediately behind this came an

Below: Mass production allowed Boeing to produce 512 B-17Es in just over nine months, with the final example rolling off the line 49 days ahead of schedule.

Above: A relatively spacious "office", the B-17 cockpit featured armoured seating for both the pilot (left) and co-pilot, and a mass of instrument dials, sticks and levers.

armour plate, then the table and chair and the port side of the forward fuselage for the navigator. Behind him, on the starboard side of the fuselage, were the oxygen bottles and a storage box for navigation instruments.

BATTLE STATIONS

The B-17 flight deck had side-by-side seating for the pilot and co-pilot. Aft of this area was the upper gun turret, normally manned by the flight engineer. Manufactured by Sperry, this weighed just under 1,000lb (454kg), and carried two .50in (12.7mm) calibre machine-guns, each with 500 rounds of ammunition. Only the upper section of the turret protruded through the aircraft skin. An electro-hydraulic system provided the power to move the turret and guns at rates of up to 45 deg/sec in azimuth and 30 deg/sec in elevation. The gunsight used in all B-17 turrets was the Sperry K-3 or K-4 mechanical rate-by-time computing unit, which compensated for angular velocity of the target.

The weapon fitted to the turret was the Browning M-2 .50in (12.7mm) machine-gun, the standard armament in all positions except the nose. The M-2 was 4ft 9in (1.45m) long, weighed 64lb (29kg), and had a nominal rate of fire of 750 rounds per minute. An electrically-powered feed carried the ammunition to the guns. Each round of ammunition was 5½in (14cm) long and weighed 1.7oz (48g). Muzzle velocity was 2,850ft/sec (869m/sec), giving a maximum effective range of 3,500ft (1,067m). The round could fly out to 21,500ft (6,557m), but lacked the power to inflict significant damage on an airframe or engine. Armour-piercing, incendiary and tracer rounds were all available for use.

A narrow door in a bulkhead aft of the dorsal turret area gave access to the bomb-bay, where the ordnance was carried vertically on bomb racks mounted on the fuselage sides and either side of a narrow central catwalk fitted with a step at its front end, and rope "railings". On long-range ferry missions, the space normally occupied by bombs was used to carry large auxiliary fuel tanks.

A small door at the aft end of the bomb-bay gave access to the radio room. This contained the radio operator's table and chair, a table-mounted radio set, and vertical racks of radio gear on either side of the door which gave access to the rear fuselage.

Below: Taking care of business in the air while the bombs did the damage far below, the M-2 .50in (12.7mm) machine-gun was a potent defensive weapon when in the hands of a skilled gunner.

Below: Displaying the lines that were to become an all-too-familiar sight in the skies over Europe, the B-17E was the first truly combat-ready model in service.

Improving the Breed

Located at the deepest point in the fuselage, the radio room was the only position in the aircraft where a tall crewman could stand upright. Incorporated within this room was a Plexiglas window with a mounting for a single .50in (12.7mm) M-2 machinegun on a ring mounting.

Another door gave access to the rear fuselage, home of the gunners. On early B-17Es, the first object aft of the radio room door was the operating mechanism of the Bendix Remote-Control Belly Turret sighting blister.

Early experience showed that gunners were having problems with the aiming periscope used to direct the turret itself. Many reported sensations of vertigo and nausea. Consequently, from the 113th B-17E onwards, the aircraft was fitted with a Sperry retractable ball turret. Suspended on a hydraulically-operated system, and mounted in the same location as the

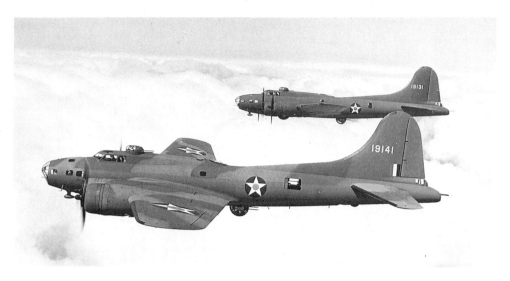

Bendix turret, this 1,290lb (586kg) assembly housed both the gunner and armament in the shape of twin .50in (12.7mm) machine-guns.

Diameter of the spherical housing was a mere 44in (112cm), so it was hardly a comfortable crew station. The gunner lay on his back, sighting the guns through the space between his open legs, while the guns themselves protruded from the powered section of the ball. Above the mounting ring which carried the ball turret were ammunition boxes, each containing 500 rounds per gun. Flexible feeds carried the rounds downward and into the rear of the ball turret.

GROUND CLEARANCE

Since clearance between the turret and the runway would be only one foot (30cm) or so, the turret could be raised partially into the fuselage, then lowered in flight. A steel door in the rear face of the turret formed part of the gunner's seat, and also served two other functions: providing armour plating to protect the gunner's back; and acting as an exit through which he could bail out in an emergency.

Aft of the ball turret were two large waist windows, each with a single

Above: Originally destined for the United Kingdom (note the RAF fin flash), the B-17E nearest to the camera was diverted to the USAAF to bolster its bomber force.

mounting carrying a .50in (12.7mm) calibre machine-gun. On the B-17E these guns had simple sights, and they were retained on the B-17F and early examples of the B-17G.

From this point back, the rear fuselage tapered sharply, leading past the wheel well cover to the most uncomfortable location in the aircraft — the tail gunner's position. At best, the tail compartment could be described as cramped and cold. The unfortunate gunner could enter either through a small door in the aft bulkhead of the tail compartment, or via a small escape hatch on the side of the fuselage, just under the starboard elevator. The twin .50in (12.7mm) machine-guns, each with 500 rounds of ammunition, protruded through the tail via a canvas boot.

Wingspan of the B-17E was 103ft 9in (31.64m); and truss-type wing spars plus an all-metal construction gave the wing the vital strength needed to absorb all flight loads, even when badly damaged. The trailing-edge flaps

Above: Shoehorned into a small compartment beneath the rudder, ''Tail-End Charlie'' — the tail gunner — was armed with a pair of .50in (12.7mm) machine-guns.

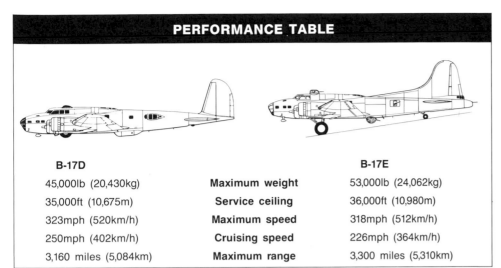

PERFORMANCE TABLE

B-17D		B-17E
45,000lb (20,430kg)	Maximum weight	53,000lb (24,062kg)
35,000ft (10,675m)	Service ceiling	36,000ft (10,980m)
323mph (520km/h)	Maximum speed	318mph (512km/h)
250mph (402km/h)	Cruising speed	226mph (364km/h)
3,160 miles (5,084km)	Maximum range	3,300 miles (5,310km)

Command was formally established, and Eaker and a six-officer staff began a six-month study of the operational techniques used by the RAF's Bomber Command against the Germans.

Aircraft losses had forced the RAF to abandon daylight bombing soon after the war began. This experience, and the less than successful operational debut of the B-17C with the RAF the previous summer, led the British to question the validity of US plans to operate the B-17E by day without fighter escort. The RAF would have preferred to see the B-17Es join in the current campaign of night bombing, and remained adamant that even this heavily-armed model would need fighter escort. No current US fighter was suitable for escort missions, so this task fell to the RAF.

By May 1942, three USAAF Bomb Groups were ready for deployment to the UK — the 92nd, 97th and 301st. First to cross the Atlantic was the 97th, which set out with its own 35 B-17Es plus 14 others from the 301st and 303rd. Two crashed in the USA, while five others made forced landings en route. The B-17 lacked the range to make the crossing directly, so they flew via Goose Bay in Labrador, Bluie West in Greenland, Reykjavik in Iceland,

were all-metal, but the ailerons were fabric-covered, as were the other flight control surfaces.

Powerplant of the B-17E was the Wright R1920-65 radial engine. Each of the four engines delivered 1,200hp at take-off, and 1,000hp at 25,000ft (7,625m). Manufactured by Hamilton Standard, the three-bladed propellers each had a diameter of 11ft 7in (3.53m). Normal internal fuel capacity was 2,490 US gal (9,425 litres), and the aircraft's oil capacity was 180 US gal (681 litres).

Early in Feburary 1942, the first B-17Es reached the hands of front-line combat units. As the 7th BG(H) B-17s were forced to move to Java, they were joined by B-17Es flown out via India. Here they operated alongside the 19th BG(H) in support of the Philippines and Java campaigns.

By April, B-17s were flying combat missions with the USAAF's 5th Air Force in Australia, and the Philippines-based 7th Air Force. They also took part in the Battle of Midway

Right: Often overshadowed by the exploits of their 8th AF cousins over Europe, Pacific-based B-17s battled it out with the Japanese, as evidenced by this "scorecard".

and the Battle of the Coral Sea. At the peak of its Pacific deployment, the B-17E would equip five Bomb Groups — the 5th, 7th, 11th, 19th and 43rd.

INTO BATTLE

Early in 1942, Hap Arnold sent Brigadier-General Ira C. Eaker to the UK to study RAF bomber operations, and to clear the way for the 8th Air Force to form under Major General Carl "Tooey" Spaatz. Eaker arrived in England on 20 Feburary. Two days later, the US Army Bomber

Improving the Breed

and Prestwick in Scotland. The first 18 reached Prestwick on 1 July.

Late July saw the 97th BG firmly installed at Polebrook and Grafton Underwood in Northamptonshire. As the unit struggled to cope with the English weather and the somewhat austere airfields, preparations began for the first combat mission.

On 17 August 18 B-17Es of the 97th BG, escorted by RAF Spitfires, headed for the coast of Northern France. While six flew a diversionary sweep along the coast, the remaining 12 attacked the Rouen-Sottevill rail marshalling yards, bombing from an altitude of 23,000ft (7,015m). All of the B-17s returned safely to base. One of the pilots assigned to the mission was Paul W. Tibbets, who three years later

would fly a Boeing B-29A Superfortress named *Enola Gay* to Hiroshima, Japan, to drop the A-bomb.

To allow the 97th BG to gain combat experience, a series of raids was planned against other French coastal targets such as Abbeville, Amiens and Dieppe. During a mission on August 21, the escorting fighters arrived late, and the nine B-17s found themselves under attack by German fighters. One aircraft was badly damaged, but all returned to base, claiming the destruction of five enemy aircraft.

For these early missions, the basic bombing formation was a six-aircraft squadron occupying a volume of sky 780ft (238m) wide, 270ft (82m) in length, and 150ft (46m) in height. Squadrons making up a formation

Above: Leaving their designated target area behind in a shroud of smoke, these B-17s maintain their tight bombing formation as they prepare to head home.

were separated by up to two miles (3.2km) laterally, 1½ miles (2.4km) in direction of flight, and 1,000ft (305m) in altitude.

During 1941, only a third of the RAF's night bombers managed to place their bombs within five miles (8km) of a target; a situation which would not improve significantly until the large-scale deployment of the *Gee* radio bombing aid in the spring of 1942. The "footprint" of the 18 aircraft making up a US Bomber Group started out at 2,340ft x 480ft (714m x 146m), so the potential accuracy of the USAAF bombing technique was more than acceptable.

The key to accurate bombing was the M-7 Norden bomb sight. By the standards of 1941, this was a complex and highly-classified item of hardware. Consisting of more than 2,000 working parts, it weighed 45lb (20kg). It was to serve until late-1943, when the improved M-9 version entered service.

The most obvious way to build a

Above: Operating from two bases in Northamptonshire, the 97th BG was tasked with carrying out the first 8th AF combat mission of the war on 17 August 1942, when B-17Es bombed targets in Rouen-Sottevill. This B-17E served with the 97th's 414th BS

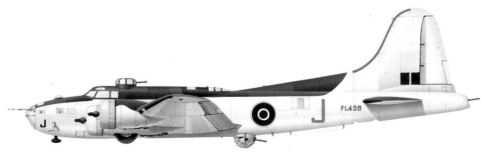

Above: Having operated the B-17C (Fortress I), the RAF acquired a batch of B-17Es for service with Coastal Command as Fortress IIs. This example served with No.220 Squadron in late 1942, scouring the Atlantic on anti-shipping and anti-submarine missions.

Left: With mainland Europe far below, widely-spaced formations of B-17s head east to another set of enemy targets.

(AA) gunners easier, any disturbance to the flight path would upset the results from the Norden sight.

Early in the combat career of the B-17, the lead bombardier in a formation was tasked with sighting for both range and deflection, while other bombardiers in the formation sighted only for range. Experience soon showed that the aircraft manoeuvres needed during the final run with the Norden sight were a potential hazard in a tightly-spaced formation in which individual bombers might be only 100ft (30.5m) or so apart.

To eliminate this problem it was decided that an experienced bombardier would be given the task of bomb-aiming for the entire formation. As he tracked the target using his Norden sight, the pilots of the other aircraft in the formation could concentrate on keeping station. When the bombs were seen to leave the lead bombardier's aircraft, the other aircraft would immediately drop their own.

bomb sight is to arrange for the optics to provide an aiming mark which will indicate the position where the bombs would impact if released at that moment in time. Sights of this type are known as "vector sights", and this technique was preferred by the RAF. Such units were simple to use, and in the stabilized form used by the RAF they allowed the pilot some leeway in manoeuvring the aircraft until just before bomb release.

An entirely different principle was used by the Norden sight (and similar units such as the British SABS and the German *Lofte*). At the heart of the Norden sight was a x 2.5 magnification aiming telescope mounted on a gyro-stabilized platform. When about a minute away from the target, the bombardier would locate his objective through the telescope, then superimpose the sight crosshairs on it. Before doing so, he would have fed information into the sight concerning the aircraft's speed and altitude, as well as ballistic information on the type of bombs to be released.

Corrections applied by the bombardier to the vertical crosshair were translated by the sight into a course correction signal which was displayed to the pilot via a simple directional indicator on the flight deck, an instrument known as the Pilot's Directional Indicator (PDI). By manipulating the vertical crosshair, the bombardier was effectively steering the aircraft. Later in the war, the Norden sight would be directly linked to the aircraft's autopilot, so that the bombardier's commands were translated directly into movements of the control surfaces.

CLOSING IN

Movement of the horizontal crosshair gave the sight information on the rate of closure to the target, and from this was deduced the range. From the slowly changing angle of the aiming telescope, the mechanical computing system in the sight was able to derive information on the aircraft's exact movement over the ground.

It was vital that the pilot keep the aircraft as steady as possible and at a constant speed for at least 20 seconds, preferably longer. Although this made the task of the German anti-aircraft

Above: For all their defensive firepower, the harsh reality for too many B-17s was death at the hands of the Luftwaffe, or anti-aircraft ground fire.

DESPITE its significant contribution to the Allied bombing campaign, the rapid escalation of the Second World War quickly rendered the B-17E all but obsolete. To maintain the USAAF's long-range bombing capabilities, a new, improved version of the Flying Fortress was soon taking shape. Not surprisingly, it was designated the B-17F; and with orders totalling no less than 3,405 examples, it would be the first B-17 variant to enter the sort of large-scale production needed to win the war against Hitler's *Festung Europa* (Fortress Europe).

Indeed, such was the scale of production that Boeing could not cope on its own. The solution lay in subcontracting the manufacture of B-17Fs out to the Douglas Aircraft Company and to Lockheed, whose respective production lines at Long Beach and Burbank (the latter having been Lockheed's Vega plant) were soon operating at full capacity to build B-17s.

Below: The B-17F also featured uprated engines, namely Wright R1820-97 Cyclones, seen here at full bore on a new B-17F during a night-time powerplant check.

The painful and protracted transition from B-17D to B-17E was not to be repeated with the new model, and B-17Fs began to flow from the three production lines in mid-1942. This tri-company organization was known officially as the Boeing-Vega-Douglas (B.V.D.) Pool. Unit costs varied, but the average price for a B-17F worked out at $357,655. Immediately recognizable by its more pointed, single-piece nose glazing, the B-17F embodied more than 400 modifications.

Above: In addition to its more pointed, one-piece nose glazing, the B-17F featured gun ports in the forward fuselage, and could carry bombs externally on inner underwing racks.

Wright R1820-97 Cyclone engines replaced the -60 model used on the B-17E, giving 1,380hp at War-Emergency setting. New paddle-bladed (wider chord) propellers were also fitted. Although more effective, these required a reprofiling of the engine nacelle cowling so as to give sufficient clearance when the wider blades were fully feathered.

New fuel tanks located in the outer wing panels allowed the carriage of more internal fuel. Known as "*Tokyo Tanks*", these gave the B-17F a maximum range of 4,220 miles (6,790km). The B-17F was also the fastest of all Flying Fortresses, with a top speed of 325mph (523km/h). In theory the aircraft could carry a bombload of up to 9,600lb (4,358kg), some weapons in the bay and the remainder on new external racks fitted between the inboard engines and the fuselage; but in practice the normal maximum war load was 4,000lb (2,816kg).

FIELD OF FIRE

The nose gun windows were increased in size to give the gunners a better field of fire, and staggered in position to give the gunners more freedom of movement. A retrofit scheme later added to production aircraft bulged these windows outward to improve the forward field of fire.

August 1942 saw the start of work on a specialized version of the B-17, the Lockheed-Vega YB-40 Flying Fortress. Conceived as the airborne equivalent of a "flack ship", this was a B-17F modified to carry an impressive selection of AA armament. By adding these aircraft to B-17 bomber formations, the USAAF hoped to improve the ability of the latter to defend themselves against the attentions of Luftwaffe fighters.

Creation of the YB-40 involved a massive upgunning of the basic B-17F airframe. To improve firepower against

Above: Though bristling with extra machine-guns, ready to blast the Luftwaffe fighters out of the sky, the YB-40's fighting potential was never fully realized in actual combat conditions.

targets approaching from above, a second Bendix dorsal turret was installed above the radio room. To cope with head-on attacks, a new turret fitted with twin .50in (12.7mm) machine-guns was fitted beneath the nose.

At the waist positions, the gun mounts were modified to accept twin .50in (12.7mm) weapons, and were given a hydraulic boost system to ease the workload of the gunners. A similar hydraulic boost was given to the tail guns, which also received a reflector sight in place of the normal ring-and-post unit. These extra guns needed their own ammunition supplies, so the number of rounds carried by the aircraft was increased to 11,275, almost three times the quantity (3,900) carried on a standard B-17F. Aircraft weight was further increased by the installation of more units of defensive armour plating.

To test the escort-Fortress concept, 23 aircraft were built by converting standard B-17Fs at the Douglas Modification Centre in Tulsa, Oklahoma, to produce a single XB-40, followed by 22 YB-40s. Flight trials started in September 1942.

Above: An internal view of the YB-40's mid-fuselage, looking aft, reveals the waist gunner ports and their bulky machine-guns. Note also the boxes of ammunition situated beneath each gun.

September also saw the pace of USAAF B-17 operations building up, with a second BG — the 301st — now in England and ready for action. The 301st received its baptism of fire on 5 September, on a bombing mission against Rouen in France. So far, the 8th AF's B-17s had suffered no losses, but luck finally ran out on the following day when the two BGs based in England pooled their strength to despatch 54 B-17Es against an aircraft factory at Meaulte in France. Two B-17s were lost to enemy fighters.

By September, the basic attack formation had been revised in an attempt to make it tighter. Two nine-aircraft squadrons were strung out in an area

Fortress v Fortress

Boeing B-17F Flying Fortress cutaway drawing key

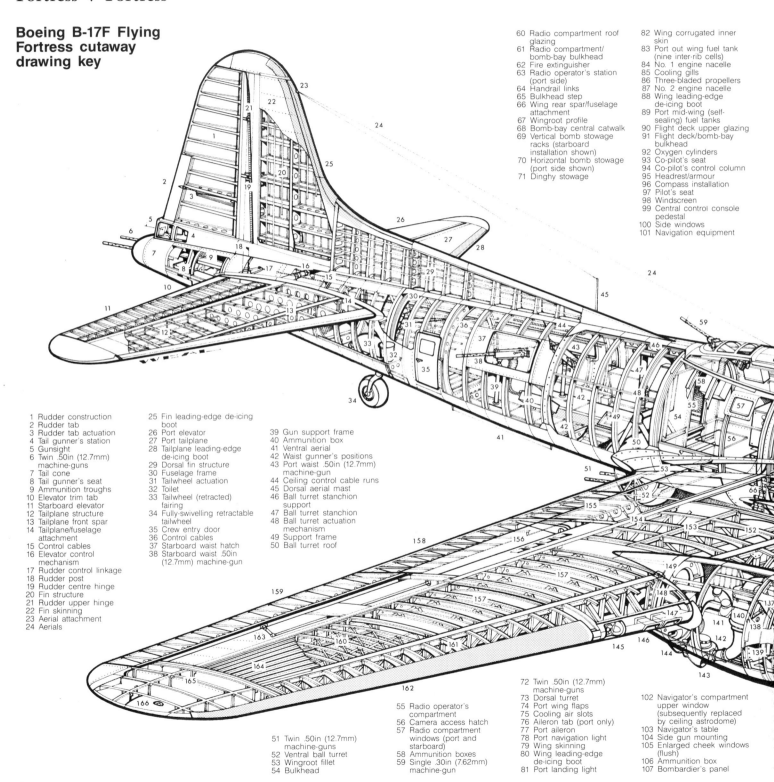

1 Rudder construction
2 Rudder tab
3 Rudder tab actuation
4 Tail gunner's station
5 Gunsight
6 Twin .50in (12.7mm) machine-guns
7 Tail cone
8 Tail gunner's seat
9 Ammunition troughs
10 Elevator trim tab
11 Starboard elevator
12 Tailplane structure
13 Tailplane front spar
14 Tailplane/fuselage attachment
15 Control cables
16 Elevator control mechanism
17 Rudder control linkage
18 Rudder post
19 Rudder centre hinge
20 Fin structure
21 Rudder upper hinge
22 Fin skinning
23 Aerial attachment
24 Aerials

25 Fin leading-edge de-icing boot
26 Port elevator
27 Port tailplane
28 Tailplane leading-edge de-icing boot
29 Dorsal fin structure
30 Fuselage frame
31 Tailwheel actuation
32 Toilet
33 Tailwheel (retracted) fairing
34 Fully-swivelling retractable tailwheel
35 Crew entry door
36 Control cables
37 Starboard waist hatch
38 Starboard waist .50in (12.7mm) machine-gun

39 Gun support frame
40 Ammunition box
41 Ventral aerial
42 Waist gunner's positions
43 Port waist .50in (12.7mm) machine-gun
44 Ceiling control cable runs
45 Dorsal aerial mast
46 Ball turret stanchion support
47 Ball turret stanchion
48 Ball turret actuation mechanism
49 Support frame
50 Ball turret roof

51 Twin .50in (12.7mm) machine-guns
52 Ventral ball turret
53 Wingroot fillet
54 Bulkhead

55 Radio operator's compartment
56 Camera access hatch
57 Radio compartment windows (port and starboard)
58 Ammunition boxes
59 Single .30in (7.62mm) machine-gun

60 Radio compartment roof glazing
61 Radio compartment/bomb-bay bulkhead
62 Fire extinguisher
63 Radio operator's station (port side)
64 Handrail links
65 Bulkhead step
66 Wing rear spar/fuselage attachment
67 Wingroot profile
68 Bomb-bay central catwalk
69 Vertical bomb stowage racks (starboard installation shown)
70 Horizontal bomb stowage (port side shown)
71 Dinghy stowage

72 Twin .50in (12.7mm) machine-guns
73 Dorsal turret
74 Port wing flaps
75 Cooling air slots
76 Aileron tab (port only)
77 Port aileron
78 Port navigation light
79 Wing skinning
80 Wing leading-edge de-icing boot
81 Port landing light

82 Wing corrugated inner skin
83 Port out wing fuel tank (nine inter-rib cells)
84 No. 1 engine nacelle
85 Cooling gills
86 Three-bladed propellers
87 No. 2 engine nacelle
88 Wing leading-edge de-icing boot
89 Port mid-wing (self-sealing) fuel tanks
90 Flight deck upper glazing
91 Flight deck/bomb-bay bulkhead
92 Oxygen cylinders
93 Co-pilot's seat
94 Co-pilot's control column
95 Headrest/armour
96 Compass installation
97 Pilot's seat
98 Windscreen
99 Central control console pedestal
100 Side windows
101 Navigation equipment

102 Navigator's compartment upper window (subsequently replaced by ceiling astrodome)
103 Navigator's table
104 Side gun mounting
105 Enlarged cheek windows (flush)
106 Ammunition box
107 Bombardier's panel

Boeing B-17 Flying Fortress

108 Norden bombsight installation
109 Plexiglas frameless nose-cone
110 Single .50in (12.7mm) machine-gun
111 Opitcally-flat bomb-aiming panel
112 Pitot head fairing (port and starboard)
113 D/F loop bullet fairing
114 Port mainwheel
115 Flight deck underfloor control linkage
116 Wingroot/fuselage fairing
117 Wing front spar/fuselage attachment
118 Battery access panels (wingroot leading-edge)
119 No. 3 engine nacelle spar bulkhead
120 Intercooler pressure duct
121 Mainwheel well
122 Oil tank (nacelle inboard wall)
123 Nacelle structure

124 Exhaust
125 Retracted mainwheel (semi-recessed)
126 Firewall
127 Cooling gills
128 Exhaust collector ring assembly
129 Three-bladed propellers
130 Undercarriage retraction struts
131 Starboard mainwheel
132 Axle
133 Mainwheel oleo leg
134 Propeller reduction gear casing
135 1,000hp Wright R-1829-65 radial engine
136 Exhaust collector ring
137 Engine upper bearers
138 Firewall
139 Engine lower bearers
140 Intercooler assembly
141 Oil tank (nacelle outboard wall)
142 Supercharger
143 Intake

144 Supercharger waste-gate
145 Starboard landing light
146 Supercharger intake
147 Intercooler intake
148 Ducting
149 No. 4 engine nacelle spar bulkhead
150 Oil radiator intake
151 Main spar web structure
152 Mid-wing fuel tank rib cut-outs
153 Auxiliary mid spar
154 Rear spar
155 Landing flap profile

156 Cooling air slots
157 Starboard outer wing fuel tank (nine inter-rib cells)
158 Flap structure
159 Starboard aileron
160 Outboard wing ribs
161 Spar assembly
162 Wing leading-edge de-icing boot
163 Aileron control linkage
164 Wing corrugated inner skin
165 Wingtip structure
166 Starboard navigation light

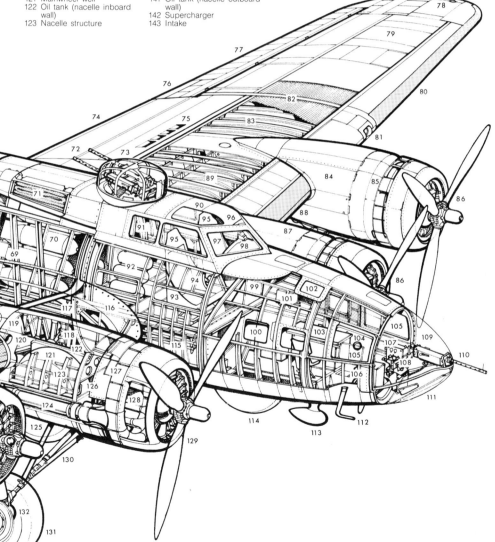

of sky 2,340ft (714m) wide and 480ft (146m) in length. The second squadron flew just behind the first, 500ft (153m) higher and echeloned towards the sun.

As the USAAF bomber effort expanded, new aircraft and Air Forces were needed. September 1942 saw the formation by General Jimmy Doolittle of the 12th AF. Operational home for the 12th AF would be the Mediterranean, where it would be used to support Operation ''*Torch*'': the Allied coastal landings in Algeria and French Morocco.

By November, the Luftwaffe had identified the greatest weakness of the B-17F — vulnerability to head-on attack. Several upgunning schemes were devised by the USAAF, such as replacing the nose-mounted .30in (7.62mm) machine-gun with a .50in (12.7mm) weapon, deliveries of the necessary modification kits starting in December. Another scheme applied to some aircraft installed twin .50in (12.7mm) guns in the nose.

During the same month the 8th AF lost two of its BGs (the 97th and 301st), which had flown 15 and nine combat missions respectively. They were now transferred to the 12th AF for operations in North Africa. Operating from Maison Blanche in Algiers, the 97th flew its first combat mission in the Mediterranean area on 16 November. By the end of 1943, the US bomber force in the UK consisted of the B-17F-equipped 91st, 303rd, 305th and 306th BGs, plus two BGs equipped with the B-24 Liberator. Experience showed that the revised bombing formation adopted in September resulted in the aircraft within a squadron blocking one another's fire due to the fact that they were all flying at the same height. In December 1942 tactics were revised, so that the 18-aircraft group now flew in a V-shaped formation slightly longer than that used earlier, and with the

Fortress v Fortress

individual aircraft stacked in echelon towards the sun. Several such groups now flew at 1½-mile (2.4km) intervals, each located above the other in a formation known as the *Javelin*.

On 20 December, six B-17s out of a total of 101 were shot down during a mission to Romilly-sur-Seine in France. The 8th AF was starting to see the sort of loss rates it might expect if and when it attempted missions beyond the range of friendly escort fighters. Curtis LeMay, now a Lieutenant Colonel and commander of the 305th BG summed up 1942 by saying: "We were a pretty sorry lot in 1942. Many people didn't live long enough to learn much." 1943 promised to be rough.

On 27 January, B-17Fs of the 91st 303rd, 305th and 306th BGs carried out the first USAAF raid on a target in Germany itself. While two B-17Fs carried out a diversionary raid on

Emden, the main force bombed the northern port of Wilhelmshaven. This was the secondary target. The attack was intended to hit the submarine yards at Vegesack, but these were concealed by clouds. Only one B-17 was lost, but the casualty rate was soon to rise significantly.

MOUNTING LOSSES

The downing of four B-17s out of a force of 86 sent to attack the railway marshalling yards at Hamm on 7 February took the loss rate close to the five per cent considered acceptable by US planners; but two missions later 16 were lost from a 106-strong force sent to attack the Forcke-Wulf aircraft works at Bremen. The loss rate fell again on later missions, but the need for better aircraft and adequate escort fighters was obvious. At this stage of the war, an individual aircrewman's chances of surviving his tour of 25 missions was only 35 per cent.

By February 1943, it had become obvious that the latter groups in a *Javelin* formation had trouble keeping up due to their higher cruising altitude. In the revised *Wedge* forma-

Above: Though she was all but cut in two by an out-of-control Bf 109 fighter, the 97th BG's "All American" somehow managed to limp home to England.

tion, the lead group flew at a medium altitude, with those following ranged at ever increasing distances above and below the leaders.

This arrangement proved short-lived. As the Luftwaffe fighter pilots grew bolder, greater firepower was needed, and this could only be provided by flying a tighter formation. In March, clusters of three groups began flying as a combat wing. Essentially

Below: Photographed in May 1943 while on her way to bomb targets in France, "Mary Ruth — Memories of Mobile" was assigned to the 401st BS, 91st BG, based at Bassingbourn, Cambridgeshire.

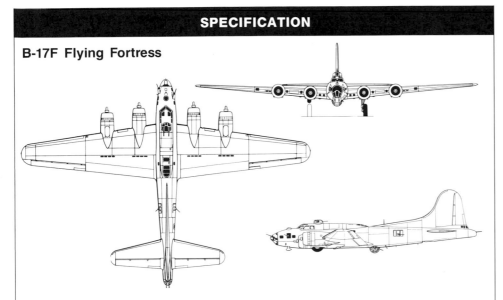

SPECIFICATION

B-17F Flying Fortress

Dimensions
Length: 74ft 9in (22.80m)
Height: 19ft 2½in (5.86m)
Wing span: 103ft 9in (31.65m)
Gross wing area: 1,420sq ft (132m²)

Weights
Empty (typical): 34,000lb (15,436kg)
Normal loaded: 56,000lb (25,424kg)
Maximum loaded: 65,500lb (29,737kg)
Maximum bombload: 9,600lb (4,358kg)
Typical ETO bombload: 4,000lb (1,816kg)

Power
4×Wright R-1820-97 Cyclone 9-cylinder, turbocharged radial piston engines, each rated at 1,200hp for take-off and 1,380hp at War-Emergency setting

Performance
Maximum speed: 325mph (523km/h)
Cruising speed: 182mph (293km/h)
Initial rate of climb: 900ft/min (275m/min)
Service ceiling: 38,500ft (11,743m)
Combat range: 1,100 miles (1,770km) with typical ETO bombload
Maximum range: 4,220 miles (6,790km)

In April 1943, four more B-17-equipped BGs arrived in England from the USA to boost the strength of the 8th AF. Released from its training role, the 92nd BG once more became an operational unit, while the return to England of the B-24s of the 93rd BG gave the 8th AF a nominal strength of around 500 aircraft, around half of which would be available for operations at any one time.

By April, the need for a better group formation saw the 18 aircraft within each individual group flying in a new formation whose V-shape was more swept. This reduced the width of each group from 2,340ft (714m) to 1,140ft (348m), but kept the length unchanged at 600ft (183m). The formation still covered just over 900ft (275m) in altitude, but instead of being ranged individually in echelon, the bombers formed three-aircraft formations which in turn flew in echelon. This revised wing formation was to last through the whole of 1943.

Below: A big brute of a machine, the Republic P-47 Thunderbolt (often simply referred to as the "Jug") would provide much-needed escort firepower for the B-17s.

a miniature *Wedge*, this had a lead group, a second group flying just behind and above, and a third group on the other side and below. The entire formation occupied a volume of sky measuring just 7,020ft (2,141m) wide, 1,800ft (549m) long, and 2,900ft (885m) in height.

To protect its bombers, the USAAF hoped to deploy new, long-range escort fighters. The first of these to arrive in the UK was the Republic P-47 Thunderbolt. Known to its pilots as the "Jug", this massive, radial-engined fighter weighed around 7 tons (7.1 tonnes), but offered a ceiling of 40,000ft (12,200m) or more, and a top speed of more than 400mph (644km/h).

Above: Flying at the head of a V-shaped formation, the lead-ship and her cohorts show just how tight the bomber formations were.

In North Africa, two more BGs — the 2nd and 99th — had joined the 12th AF, supplementing the 97th and 301st BGs which had been there since late-1942. Fortresses from all four units were used to attack targets in the Western Mediterranean.

Back in England, May 1943 had seen the long-awaited combat debut of the vitally-needed escort fighters on which the 8th AF was relying. On 4 May, P-47s escorted the bombers during an attack against the Ford vehicle works at Antwerp, Belgium. When carrying 100 US gal (378.5 litre) wing fuel tanks, the Thunderbolts had enough range to cross the Dutch/German border.

By now, the Luftwaffe had realized the need for even more firepower on its fighters; and in May, a special anti-bomber trials unit was set up at Witt-

Right: While the 8th AF operated from the United Kingdom, 12th AF units, including the 99th BG, operated from bases located in the Mediterranean region.

mundhafen. This included a Zerstörergeschwader (ZG: Destroyer Group) commanded by Hauptmann Eduard Tratt, and equipped with 10 Bf 110s, a single Messerschmitt Me 210 and two of the new Me 410s. These were used to test 1.45in (37mm) and 2in (50mm) cannon, as well as 3in (8cm), 8.2in (21cm) and 11.8in (30cm) unguided rockets.

In the meantime, Luftwaffe fighter pilots did their best to exploit the B-17's weak nose armament, with nearly three-quarters of their attacks now being flown head-on. Although the gun turrets could provide some degree of fire in the forward sector to supplement the nose-mounted guns, none of the B-17's armour was positioned to provide protection against frontal attack.

As the summer wore on, the intensity of B-17 operations mounted, with increasing numbers of aircraft being despatched on missions. Inevitably, there was an increase in the number of aircraft lost in action. On 22 June, 257 B-17s hit the synthetic rubber factory at Huls in the Ruhr Valley. Ac-

cording to the USAAF, 88 per cent of the bombs fell inside the plant area, and 47 enemy fighters were claimed as "kills". But the Germans managed to down 20 B-17s.

HEAVY METAL

By now, the YB-40 escort Flying Fortress was ready for combat. Ferried to England in early May, the YB-40s were assigned to the 92nd BG at Alconbury, Huntingdonshire. The first combat mission was flown on 27 May, when seven YB-40s took part in a raid on the French port of St. Nazaire. They were to prove a failure. By early July, nine missions had been flown, and the combat deficiencies of the YB-40 concept had become all too apparent. Due to its extra weight, the modified aircraft was awkward to control, and was slower than a standard B-17F. During combat missions, the YB-40s had difficulty in keeping up with the bombers they were supposed to protect, particularly once the latter had dropped their bombs, while the presence of a handful of extra aircraft

Left: Rugged and reliable from the outset, the B-17's success nevertheless relied to a large extent on the skills and labours of highly dedicated groundcrew to keep them "fighting fit".

Below: With twelve sorties to her credit, "Lil" awaits the loading of the bombs for her next flight. A typical B-17F European Theatre of Operations bombload weighed in at 4,000lb (1,816kg).

each with six more guns added little to the combined firepower of a massive B-17 formation.

Only one feature of the unsuccessful YB-40 escort Flying Fortress had appealed to the 8th AF –– its chin turret. It may have been the end of the line for the ill-conceived YB-40, but it was the start of big business for Bendix. That chin turret was to be a feature of the new B-17G, the final and most widely-produced version of the Boeing B-17 Flying Fortress family.

FURTHER DEVELOPMENT

The prototype B-17G was created by taking a B-17F from the production line and fitting it with the new chin turret, plus other minor modifications such as a revised navigator's station and better actuators for the bomb racks and bomb-bay doors. By the late summer of 1943, the new variant was being phased in on all three of the B-17 production lines.

July 1943 ended with "Blitz Week". Between 24 and 30 July, the 8th AF flew six bombing missions, and 16

targets were bombed, including the Focke-Wulf plants at Warnemunde and Oschersleben. The latter mission — flown on the 28th — was the deepest penetration into Germany to date, and was made possible by the fuel tanks fitted in the outer wing sections of the B-17F. A total of 84 Fortresses had been lost, for the claimed loss of 296 enemy fighters. Total score for the month was 128 B-17s lost, for the claimed downing of 545 fighters. Actual Luftwaffe losses were 40!

On 17 August, the first anniversary of the initial B-17 mission to Rouen, the 8th AF launched its first attack against two targets located deeper in Germany than had ever been attempted before. Regensburg was the home of a Messerschmitt works so was obviously a major target; but Schwein-

Above: Compared to the B-17F nose at left, the B-17G was easily recognizable thanks to the chin turret, a legacy of the abandoned YB-40 project.

Fortress v Fortress

Above: Bombs away! High over German soil, B-17Fs deliver some of the 18,925 tons of bombs dropped by the 94th BG during the Second World War.

furt had been identified as the main German manufacturing source of ball bearings. Knock out Schweinfurt, planners argued, and production of all kinds of sophisticated weaponry would be badly hampered.

A force of 376 B-17s was despatched on schedule, but early-morning fog delayed the take-off of the P-47 escorts. By the time that the Regenburg force reached its target, 14 bombers had already been lost. After releasing their bombs and inflicting massive damage on one of the Messerschmitt factories, the remaining 132 did not return to England but flew south to land in North Africa, making this the first-ever ''shuttle'' mission to be flown by the 8th AF. During this southward leg of the long flight, ten more B-17s were brought down by the Germans.

In all, the two missions had cost the 8th AF 60 aircraft, plus more than 100 damaged. Post-mission inspection caused 35 of the damaged aircraft to be written off as beyond repair.

Several days later, the Regensburg raiders left their temporary North African bases and flew back to England, bombing the Focke-Wulf works at Bordeaux en route. Around 40 aircraft were lost.

LIMITED SUCCESS

Knocking out the Luftwaffe by destroying aircraft production plants was never a practical proposition. German production of fighters had increased steadily from the spring of 1942 onwards, peaking at just over 2,400 per month in July 1943. This fell to under 2,100 in August, but by then a programme to disperse aircraft production facilities was under way.

By now, the new B-17G was in production, and the first example was handed over to the USAAF on 4 September 1943. The Douglas and Locheed-Vega lines also switched to the new variant, although the first 76 Douglas-built examples retained the B-17F designation within the company. Nevertheless the USAAF referred to them as B-17Gs.

Above: Based at Bassingbourn, the 91st BG — know affectionately as the "Ragged Irregulars" — was to claim 420 enemy aircraft

for 197 B-17s lost, both the highest figures in the 8th AF. Luck ran out for this 322nd BS B-17F on 6 September 1943, over Stuttgart.

Subsequent modifications were minor, so the aircraft retained the B-17G designation through its production run. Many of the changes were intended to help the crew, as well as to improve survivability and maintainability. For example, the cockpit instrumentation was improved; the engine fire-extinguishing system was upgraded; an emergency oil supply for propeller feathering was added; and the engine turbo-superchargers were changed from hydraulic to electric control. Other changes saw windows fitted to the waist gunner's positions, followed by a staggering of the position of these apertures to lessen the

Above: Wearing the code letters of the 359th BS, 303rd BG, at Molesworth during summer 1943, this B-17F also sports a medium

green mottle atop its olive drab camouflage. The 303rd would go on to become the first 8th AF BG to complete 300 missions.

risk of one waist gunner getting in the other's way.

On 27 September, P-47s with underwing fuel tanks were able to accompany B-17s all the way to Emden. That same day, Allied ground forces moving north through Italy captured a complex of 13 air bases around Foggia. USAAF bombers swiftly occupied these airfields, and on 1 October flew their first mission from their new homes — a mission against Wiener Neustadt.

By now, the B-17G had arrived in Europe; but on 4 October, the USAAF recorded its first B-17G losses when two Douglas-built examples failed to return from a raid against targets in Germany. The new model had arrived just in time for use in "Big Week". This commenced on 8 October, when 399 aircraft — the largest number ever despatched — were sent to attack Bremen and other targets. Later raids hit Anklam, the Focke-Wulf manufacturing plant at Marienburg, and Gdynia.

The climax of "Big Week" came on 14 October with a second raid on Schweinfurt. Here the USAAF was to meet another new Luftwafe anti-bomber weapon: the Fw 190A-4/R6 toting a pair of 8.2in (21cm) unguided rockets under the wings. Fired from outside the defensive range of the bombers' .50in (12.7mm) machine-guns, these explosive-packed projectiles were used to break up a formation so that large numbers of conventional fighters could engage the individual bombers. Trials of the system earlier that year had shown that from a range of 3,280ft (1,000m), rounds had a deviation of plus or minus 130ft (40m) in the horizontal plane, and plus or minus 23ft (7m) in the vertical.

Like the big 2in (50mm) cannon, this weapon required a heavily loaded fighter to fly a long tail chase against its quarry until within firing range, making the fighter a vulnerable

target for the USAAF fighter escorts. In the long term, such tactics were near suicidal, but in the skies above Germany that day, they worked. B-17 losses were heavy. Of the 291 B-17s sent out, 45 were shot down, a further 17 crashed in the UK before landing, while at least 17 more were damaged beyond repair. One source suggests that around 30 per cent of the 121 damaged aircraft were written off. German losses were 38 fighters lost, 51 badly damaged. However, German ball-bearing production was cut by 67 per cent, and fighter production subsequently fell in November to less than 1,900 aircraft in total.

NEW ARRIVALS

Late in November 1943, the 401st BG arrived at Deenthorpe in Norfolk. It was the first unit to be equipped from scratch with the B-17G, and it was active by the end of the month. Another new arrival was an intitial batch of P-38J Lightnings, the first model of this fighter to be fitted with supercharged engines.

Despite such arrivals, 1943 was ending in near-disaster for the 8th AF, although December saw the first missions flown by the P-51B Mustang. The 354th FG, a 9th AF unit on loan to the 8th AF, flew its first short-range sortie on 1 December, and its first escort mission on 5 December during a raid on Amiens. On the 15th, a mixed force of P-38s and P-51s escorted 8th AF B-17s all the way to Kiel, and the next day the 354th FG scored its first confirmed victory. With the P-51 now flying over German territory, 1944 promised to be a better year.

Below: With the twists and turns of the duelling fighters forming an impressive backdrop in the sky above Europe, B-17Fs assigned to the 390th BG hold formation and press on toward another set of targets in German territory.

IN combat, the USAAF B-17s were flown in large formations, the aim of which was to provide a degree of mutual protection. However, studies carried out in 1943 showed all too clearly that around one half of the Flying Fortresses lost in combat had left their formation. Given the choice of attacking a tight formation or a single bomber out on its own, who could blame the Luftwaffe fighter pilots for choosing the latter?

The hard truth was that a B-17 forced to leave its formation due to battle damage or engine failure stood little chance of surviving. The best tactic was for the stragglers to form their own slower-flying formation.

Early in 1944, the standard combat bomber formation was revised once

Below: Constantly harassed by Luftwaffe fighters, the B-17s also had to endure the lethal ''flak'' sent skywards courtesy of anti-aircraft artillery (AAA) units.

Above: Further revision of the standard formation led to the B-17s flying even closer to each other in an attempt to maximize their defensive firepower.

more in an effort to tighten it up still further. The goal now was not to maximize defensive firepower — the fighter escorts were available to deal with the marauding Luftwaffe fighters — but to provide the escort fighters with the smallest possible volume of sky to defend.

A new 36-aircraft formation, made up of three clusters with 12 B-17s each, replaced the standard 18-strong grouping. The clusters flew in a V-shaped echelon formation, with all 36 bombers packed into a volume of sky just 1,560ft (476m) wide, 810ft (247m) long, and 600ft (183m) deep. Groups no longer flew in their traditional wing-sized *Wedge* formations, but followed one another at four-mile (6.4km) intervals at the same altitude.

Throughout the rest of the war, the density of the B-17 bomber formation was gradually tightened to the point where 54 Flying Fortresses making up a Combat Wing formation shared a

block of sky only 2,850ft (869m) wide, 1,275ft (389m) long, and 2,700ft (824m) deep.

In February 1944, the USAAF carried out a brief campaign intended to destroy the five main production centres of German fighters. Codenamed Operation *"Argument"*, this was an ambitious plan, and one on which the USAAF was prepared to expend up to two-thirds of its long-range bomber force of B-17s and B-24s.

Operation *"Argument"* started on 20 February, when 1,028 aircraft attacked Leipzig in Germany for the loss of only 26. By the standards of late-1943, this 2½ per cent loss rate was comfortably acceptable. Over the next five days, attacks by UK-based B-17s and the Italian-based 15th AF led to the loss of a further 226 USAAF B-17 and B-24 bombers.

22 February saw the deployment of P-51Bs with the 9th AF's 363rd FG. Five days later, the P-51B/Cs needed

Above: Bearing the ''6G'' code of the RAF's No.223 Squadron, based at Oulton, Norfolk, this was one of 98 B-17Gs supplied to the RAF as Fortress IIIs. Redesignated as a B.III, this machine was used on covert intelligence gathering and electronic jamming missions.

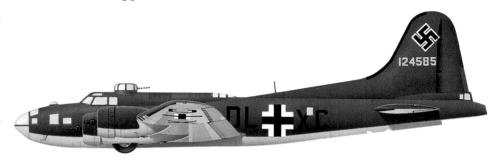

Below: With so many bombers in such close proximity, accidents did happen. This aircraft was lost after a newly-dropped bomb sheared off its port tailplane.

Above: Definitely an unofficial ''customer'' for the B-17, Germany managed to get its hands on this ex-303rd BG B-17F after it was forced down over France. Initially used for demonstration purposes (as shown), it was subsequently repainted in dark camouflage and used on clandestine missions by the Luftwaffe's I/KG 200.

to equip the 4th FG, the 8th AF's first Mustang unit, were handed over. On the following day, despite the fact that its pilots averaged less than one hour of flying time on the new fighter, the unit flew its first combat mission: the start of more than 1.1 million combat flying hours by European-based Mustangs. With two P-51B/C production lines running in the USA, the new fighter would arrive in Europe at the rate of around 100 a month from now on.

In February, the RAF deployed its first B-17Gs. Known as Fortress IIIs, these were reworked by Scottish Aviation at Prestwick, Scotland, for service with No. 100 Group. Formed on 8 November 1943, this would be the

The Campaign Continues

world's first specialized electronic warfare (EW) unit. The Fortress III was intended for night operations, so its engines were fitted with flame-damping mufflers. A large radome under the nose housed the RAF's standard H2S navigation/target-finding radar, while the bomb bay was sealed and converted into an internal avionics bay.

RADIO JAMMERS

Here were located the Fortress III's electronic "weapons". Each aircraft received eight *Mandrel* jammers designed to counter German search radars, and an *Airborne Cigar* Very High Frequency (VHF) communications jammer able to interfere with Luftwaffe air-to-ground radio links. The latter system was replaced by the higher-powered and more effective *Jostle IV*. To operate this equipment, two extra crewmen were carried.

A similar programme saw 11 8th AF B-17s fitted out as EW aircraft. Later joined by two B-17Gs, these aircraft carried various types of EW equipment, including *Mandrel* and *Carpet* radar jammers, as well as some early forms of electronic intelligence (Elint) gathering equipment.

By now the B-17G greatly outnumbered the F-model in Europe. February also saw the arrival in the UK of the first unpainted B-17Gs, the result of a December 1943 USAAF decision to abandon the use of camouflage. Most early natural metal Fortresses went to Mediterranean units, starting with the 463rd and 483rd BGs based at Celone and Tortorella respectively; but on 13 March, the 457th BG became the first 8th AF unit to fly a "silver" formation on a combat mission.

Crews assigned to natural metal aircraft were initially worried that Luftwaffe fighter pilots might single them

out for attack, so many units tried to wait until enough unpainted B-17s were available to form a formation before committing these to action. By the summer, "silver" Fortresses outnumbered their olive-drab counterparts, although a few of the latter survived the war.

March 1944 was to prove a crisis point for both sides. In that month, the USAAF mounted five missions against Berlin. During the third mission, on 6 March, the 8th AF lost 69 aircraft — its highest-ever loss in a single day. Despite such losses, the Luftwaffe was badly mauled. March 1944 also saw the arrival in quantity of the first P-51D Mustangs for 8th AF units. In future, the B-17s and B-24s

Below: As 1944 progressed, the standard olive drab camouflage gave way to natural metal and more colourful unit markings, as seen on these 447th BG B-17Gs.

Above: Scourge of the Luftwaffe from early-1944 onwards, the P-51D Mustang long-range escort fighter helped reduce the B-17's vulnerability to fighter attack.

could be escorted all the way to Berlin by a fighter equally as agile as its Luftwaffe counterparts.

MIXED FORCE

By April, the USAAF was able to despatch up to 1,000 bombers against targets. This month also saw the arrival in England of the last US BG to be deployed overseas. Originally formed as a training unit for replacement crews, the 398th BG was equipped with B-17Gs and despatched to the UK. Starting in April 1944, the 8th AF's 3rd Bombardment Division (BD) began to operate some B-24s. By the summer, the 34th, 486th, 487th, 490th and 493rd and BGs all operated the Liberator, while the other nine units operated with B-17s. On 14 April, all strategic bombers in Europe were placed under the command of Supreme Headquarters, Allied Expeditionary Force (SHAEF) in advance of

Operation "Overlord" — the Allied invasion of Normandy, France.

By now a campaign was also under way to attack the German oil industry. A major target was the oil fields at Ploesti in Romania, thought to be producing some 30 per cent of the Axis' oil supplies. These had been attacked by B-24s in August 1943, but a new series of strikes sent B-17s against Ploesti for the first time. The new attacks started with three attacks by the B-24s of the 15th AF, the first of which was flown on 5 April. First participation by 8th AF B-17s and B-24s was on 12 May, when almost 900 aircraft bombed six targets at Ploesti.

On 2 July the Me 410-equipped ZG 76, supported by Bf 109Gs and Bf 110s, claimed 34 bombers and 11 other aircraft (presumably fighters) during an air battle over Budapest, Hungary. No Me 410s were lost in this action, but the type was rarely so successful.

By the summer of 1944, Boeing's production line at Seattle had hit a peak production rate of 16 B-17G every 24 hours. Average weekly losses due to combat and accidents were about 60 B-17s. Only a handful of B-17Fs remained in service in the UK, though some were to soldier on in the Mediterranean theatre.

As had been the case in the Mediterranean, operating a mix of B-17s and B-24s in a single BD created problems, both in the air as a result of their differing performance, and on the ground due to the logistical and support demands of a second type of aircraft. In June and July, the five B-24 Groups in the 8th AF's 3rd BD traded in their B-24s for B-17Gs, making the 8th AF an all-Flying Fortress establishment. The last unit to convert was the 34th BG.

B-17Gs arriving in Europe from June 1944 onwards featured a revised

Below: A moment's respite for a pair of outbound 91st BG B-17s, as a twin-engined Messerschmitt Bf 110 interceptor peels away. But he'll be back . . .

The Campaign Continues

Above: Easily identified by the limited glazing and extended rear fuselage, the original tail gun configuration was superceded in 1944 by a new, improved unit.

Above: Designed at the United Air Lines Modification Center located in Cheyenne, Wy., the revised tail turret offered greater gun elevation and improved glazing.

tail position. Known as the *Cheyenne* tail, it had been devised by the United Air Lines Modification Center at Cheyenne, Wyoming. It slightly increased the length of the B-17, but gave the tail gunner better windows, replaced the original ring-and-bead sight with a modern reflector unit, and allowed a wider field of fire. Modification kits were devised for older aircraft, and shipped overseas. By early 1945, all 8th AF Flying Fortresses had been converted, and many kits had been shipped to the 15th AF's B-17-equipped units.

June saw a return to the concept of ''shuttle'' missions in a series of operations codenamed *Frantic*. A force of 130 15th AF B-17s attacked rail targets in Hungary on 2 June, then flew east to land at airfields near Kiev in the Soviet Union. Two days later, the bombers flew from their temporary Soviet bases to bomb an airfield in Romania, then returned to the Soviet Union. A week later, the force set off on the return flight, bombing another Romanian airfield en route.

Only two aircraft were lost, so plans were made to repeat the exercise using 8th AF aircraft. On 21 June, 163 B-17s escorted by P-51 Mustangs left

the UK, bombed a synthetic oil plant south of Berlin, then flew eastward to the Soviet Union. The bombers landed at Poltava and Mirgorod, the fighters at Piryatin.

GROUND ATTACKS

Unfortunately, the USAAF was not the only air arm to have noted the effectiveness of the shuttle mission flown earlier in the month. Five hours after

Below: Closely shadowed by two 325th FG P-51B Mustangs, this 99th BG B-17G was photographed while participating in a shuttle mission to the Soviet Union.

landing, the B-17s were attacked by a force of Heinkel He 111 and Junkers Ju 88 bombers. In strikes against the two airfields, the Luftwaffe destroyed 44 USAAF aircraft and damaged 26 more. When added to the losses suffered by other 8th AF B-17 units tasked with conventional bombing missions that day, this took the daily loss rate to an all-time high of 88 B-17s. The survivors flew south to Italy, after bombing a Polish oil plant, then attacked a rail yard in France during the final homeward leg.

Two more *Frantic* shuttle missions were flown in the weeks which followed, but the concept was then abandoned as being too dangerous. The risk

Above: Though no mission could be called easy, the longer the war continued, the greater were the chances of a B-17 crew making it through their tour of duty.

that the Luftwaffe might repeat its successful strikes against the Soviet bases was very real.

In addition to its normal bombing missions against Germany, the 8th AF flew many tactical sorties in support of the Allied invasion of Normandy by Allied bombers. By this stage of the war, the survival rate of B-17 aircrew had doubled from the poor figures of early-1943. Given that an individual crew member's chances of surviving a 25-sortie tour were now 70 per cent, the USAAF "moved the goalposts". Following D-Day, crews were now expected to fly 30 sorties — the number faced by their RAF counterparts. Despite the effect on aircrew morale, the normal tour was soon raised again, this time to 35 missions.

By the spring of 1944, the mid-1943 German decision to disperse aircraft production was finally beginning to pay off. Previously aircraft production had been tackled by 27 large plants. Now a network of 729 smaller factories was building airframes, engines and other components at an ever-in-creasing rate. This was an inefficient way to build aircraft, since it diluted the pool of trained manpower, but it provided a respite from air attack. Despite the effects of the Allied bombing campaign, monthly fighter production in March 1944 had matched its previous peak of July 1943, and was to climb steadily in the months which followed, reaching a peak of around 4,300 a month in July and September, with minimal loss of overall product quality.

Fighter production included two new types which posed a significant threat to USAAF bomber operations: the rocket-powered Messerschmitt Me 163 Komet, and the twin-turbojet Me 262. Both aircraft were known to Allied Intelligence, and on 20 July, bombing raids were mounted against airfields believed to be bases for these new aircraft.

The first Me 262 fighter unit, the Erprobungskommando 262 (Test Detachment 262), had been set up in April, and had already downed several

Below: Luckily for the Allies, Germany never did make full use of the jet-powered Messerschmitt Me 262 as an interceptor to counter the B-17 formations.

The Campaign Continues

RAF and USAAF reconnaissance aircraft. When an RAF photo-reconnaissance Mosquito returned to base on 25 July and reported having come under attack from an Me 262, it became clear that the new Luftwaffe fighters were indeed operational.

ROCKET FIGHTER

Preparations to deploy the smaller Me 163 had been under way since May, when the first squadron of Jagdgeschwader 400 (JG: Fighter Group 400) had been formed at Wittmundhafen, but its aircraft were not delivered until July. On 28 July, five Me 163s of 1/JG400 made a rear attack against 8th AF bombers operating near Merseburg. No hits were scored,

Below: A seasoned veteran of the skies over Germany, ''Little Miss Mischief'' managed to limp home to a crash-landing after being hit. The damage was not mortal, and she was soon back in action.

but the tiny, delta-winged aircraft easily eluded the P-51D escort fighters flown by the 359th FG. The next day, a 497th FG Lightning claimed an Me 163, but post-war examination of Luftwaffe air combat records showed that none were lost on that day.

The sheer speed of the Me 163 gave Luftwaffe pilots only a few seconds between coming into effective gun range and having to jink to avoid their bomber target. As a result, their success rate was low. By August, the Allies realized that the aircraft's range and endurance were very short, so bomber routes tried to avoid flying too near to known Me 163 bases.

August saw the USAAF's B-17 inventory reach its peak of 4,574. Total number deployed for operational service was 2,263: 1,829 with the 8th AF, 366 with 15th AF, and 68 outside Europe. The remaining 2,311 were still in the continental United States, either with the 23 training squadrons, or held in reserve at modification and storage centres.

Above: Another of the Luftwaffe's new generation of fighters, the Me 163 was small but potentially lethal. But again, its potential was never fully realized.

Combat sightings of the Me 163 and Me 262 increased in that month, and the escort fighters struggled to master the new threat. On 28 August, however, an Me 262 attached to Kampfgeschwader 51 (KG: Bomber Group 51) was shot down by two P-47 Thunderbolts from the 82nd FS.

At first the Me 262 was not a great success. The first full-scale interceptor unit formed on 3 October with 30 serviceable aircraft. By the end of the month it had claimed 22 ''kills', but attrition (mostly due to crashes) had reduced its force strength to only three operational aircraft.

Many Me 262s were used as fighter-bombers, but III/JG 7 — the first dedicated jet fighter unit — was formed in early December. By the end of the war, it had claimed a total of 427 ''kills'', including no less than 300 four-engined bombers.

In the final months of 1944, the Luftwaffe was able to field growing numbers of fighters as a result of the massive production figures of the summer and autumn. Shortages of fuel, spare parts and trained aircrew were the limiting factors rather than aircraft numbers. Operational availability of

the Me 163 had never been high, with only 237 delivered by the end of the year, but shortage of pilots and rocket fuel, plus attacks against known Me 163 bases caused rocket fighter operations to taper off in late-1944.

FIREPOWER CHANGES

On B-17Gs built after August 1944, the ring mounting for the radio room .50in (12.7mm) machine-gun was replaced by an alternative mounting. This modification was short-lived; in late-1944, the radio operator's Browning was deleted on new production aircraft. Protruding through the upper amidships hatch, this weapon had always been of minimal usefulness. Studies had also shown that the two

Below: Resplendent in silver and red, these 381st BG B-17Gs display the late-war revision of the dorsal armament, namely the deletion of the radio operator's .50in (12.7mm) machine-gun.

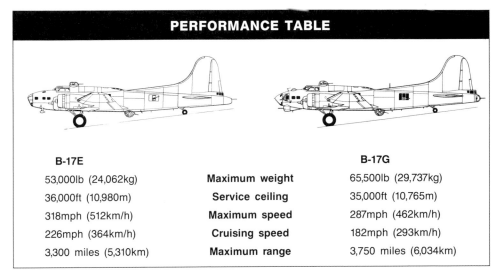

PERFORMANCE TABLE

B-17E		B-17G
53,000lb (24,062kg)	Maximum weight	65,500lb (29,737kg)
36,000ft (10,980m)	Service ceiling	35,000ft (10,765m)
318mph (512km/h)	Maximum speed	287mph (462km/h)
226mph (364km/h)	Cruising speed	182mph (293km/h)
3,300 miles (5,310km)	Maximum range	3,750 miles (6,034km)

waist gunners seldom fired at the same time, so from now on only a single waist gunner was carried. These changes lightened the aircraft and moved its centre of gravity forward by at least 5in (12.6cm). Given that the B-17 had been tail-heavy since the E-model, the changes resulted in improved aircraft handling.

Empty weight of a B-17G was about 2,135lb (969kg) more than that of a B-17F. This reduced the maximum speed in level flight at 25,000ft (7,625m) from 299mph (481km/hr) to 287mph (462km/h), and cut almost 2,000ft (610m) off the service ceiling. The winter of 1944/45 saw the installation of more powerful turbo-super-

The Campaign Continues

chargers in order to improve high-altitude performance.

By early-1945, aircraft were being fitted with an electrically-operated handgrip on the control column. Known as the "Formation Stick", this reduced the effort needed to maintain a tight formation at altitude.

By the end of the war, the B-17 was used as the basis for several specialized types of aircraft. Some F- and G-model aircraft whose equipment shortages made them unfit for regular combat duties were reassigned to the weather-reconnaissance role, while some B-17Fs were converted as long-range reconnaissance aircraft. Three versions were built for the latter role: the F-9A, -9B and -9C. These could carry 6in (15.2cm) trimetrogon, 6in (15.2cm) and 12in (30.4cm) vertical, and 6in (15.2cm) oblique cameras.

Such was the pace of combat operations, that many B-17s were retired as "War Weary" — unfit for further combat operations. These veterans were obvious candidates for other roles. Under a project known as *Aphrodite*, 10 war-weary B-17E and -17F bombers were stripped of armament in the autumn of 1944, and fitted out with radio control systems to enable them to be used as guided missiles. Packed with up to 10 tons (10.6 tonnes) of high explosives, and escorted by one of a number of B-17s modified to act as control ships, these BQ-17s (later BQ-17Gs) were designed to be quite literally crashed into suitable German targets.

PROJECT CASTOR

Under a follow-on project known as *Castor* a further 20 old B-17E and -17F bombers were put through a similar rebuild which used a more sophisticated control arrangement. This involved installing a nose-mounted RC-489 TV system, an ARW-1 remote control radio system linked to the

Above: In an attempt to improve the chances of accurate bombing in adverse weather conditions, some B-17Gs carried an H2S Bombing Through Overcast (BTO) radar in place of the ball turret.

flight controls, plus a radio beacon and smoke-dispensing system intended to serve as tracking aids. Packed with around nine tons (9.14 tonnes) of *Torpex* explosive, 11 of these flying bombs were deployed for combat.

Project *Castor* envisaged the use of B-17 drones in an attack on the German Navy's battleship *Tirpitz,* then hiding in the Norwegian fjords. The use of torpedo-like bombs too long for conventional loading necessitated the radical modification of a B-17F. With the rear fuselage essentially removed, and with an open cockpit for the two-man crew, this extremely sleek-looking machine was soon appropriately nicknamed the "B-17 *Roadster*". The RAF got to the *Tirpitz* first, however, and this one-off version of the Flying Fortress was not used operationally.

With the first target accounted for, the U-boat pens at Heligoland in Norway became the new target. On 11 September, a BQ-17 packed with 18,425lb (8,364kg) of *Torpex* was

shepherded towards this target, only to be shot down short of its final destination. Tragically, one of the crew was killed whilst bailing out.

A pair of BQ-17s were subsequently despatched to destroy the oil refinery at Henningstadt, but the mission failed. On 15 October, another pair of drones took to the air, this time with the support buildings at Heligoland as their target. One of the aircraft was lost to German gunnery short of the target; but the other went on to score a direct hit, exploding with devastating results on impact. Finally, a mission had ended in success.

Two more BQ-17s were launched on 31 October, and the final *Castor* operation was conducted on 5 December. This last mission again involved a pair of drones, and again one of them was shot down before reaching its target. The second aircraft, however, suffered icing problems and crash-landed without blowing-up. German troops surrounded the aircraft and, unaware the aircraft was unmanned, demanded that the crew surrender. When no response was forthcoming from inside the BQ-17, the Germans promptly opened fire. The resulting explosion created a crater 20ft (6m) in depth. Fittingly, the

Above: In addition to regular 500lb (227kg) "iron" bombs, a variety of more specialized ordnance, such as these smaller fragmentation bombs, were dropped by B-17s during the war.

BQ-17 "flying-bomb" programme had come to and with a bang.

Six retired B-17Gs were modified early in 1945 to act as rescue aircraft able to drop a lifeboat to ditched aircrew. Several successful sorties were flown in March 1945, and this led to six new B-17Gs being given a similar modification. Designated B-17H, the aircraft also featured an ASR search radar mounted in place of the B-17G's chin gun turret.

The Battle of the Bulge — Germany's counter-attack through the French Ardennes in December 1944 — placed Allied ground forces temporarily on the defensive, and the USAAF bomber force was ordered to intervene. For ten days, the 8th AF flew tactical missions against German units, dropping almost 100,000 tons (101,600 tonnes) of bombs. A mission flown on 24 December involved 2,055 bombers and 1,024 fighters — the largest single air attack mounted during the Second World War.

As the Allies advanced into Germany, the 8th and 15th AFs flew supporting missions, bombing from altitudes of around 10,000ft (3,050m) in order to maximize accuracy.

By now, German fighter production was beginning to fall off. The dispersal system made aircraft factories difficult to find and attack, but the bottleneck in such a system was the

Below: Another mission underway for a quartet of 91st BG B-17Gs. The unit was the first to complete 100 missions during the war, and dropped just over 22,000 tons of bombs on enemy targets.

need to transport sub-assemblies and completed aircraft. As the result of air attack and shortage of fuel, delivery figures started to collapse.

BOMBING LEGACY

Fighter deliveries in January 1945 had been an impressive 2,600, but very few Me 163s were included. In February, this figure fell to around 1,700. The March figure was around 1,300, but this was the end of the line for an industry which had performed near-miracles under heavy bombardment. In April, deliveries fell to less than 100 fighters.

The Campaign Continues

Even the Me 262 was finding it hard to survive in skies effectively ruled by Allied fighters. On 25 February, 16 of the jet fighters taking off from an airfield near Wurzburg were jumped by 38th FS P-51Ds. Seven Me 262s were lost and three pilots killed, including the commander of the Me 262 unit. February also saw the conversion of I/JG 1 from the Fw 190 to the last of Germany's new fighters, the single-engined Heinkel He 162 Volksjager "People's Fighter", but there are no verified reports of this aircraft being engaged in combat.

New types of weapon were also being tested by the 8th and 15th AFs. The VB-1 *Azon* was a 1,000lb (45kg) bomb modified by the addition of a 164lb (74kg) tail section containing an ARW-10 radio receiver, gyroscopes and movable tail surfaces. This allowed the weapon to be steered in azimuth to correct its eventual point of impact by up to 200ft (61m).

The *Disney* rocket-boosted bomb was intended for use against the thick concrete rooves of U-boat pens. Developed by Britain's Royal Navy, the 4,500lb (2,043kg) weapon was 14ft (4.27m) long, and a difficult load for British bombers to carry. Following trial releases from a B-17G in the autumn of 1944, the bomb made its combat debut on 14 March 1945 when the 8th AF's 92nd BG dropped several such weapons on the U-boat pens at Ijmuiden, on the Dutch coast.

The final new air-launched weapon to be tried by the B-17 was the GB-1 glide bomb: an M34 2,000lb (908kg) bomb fitted with wings, a tail and an automatic stabilizer. Tried in action on a raid against Cologne, it proved inaccurate, being easily disturbed by wind. It was followed by a TV-guided version known as the BG-4.

As Luftwaffe fighter strength plummeted, B-17 units began to trade firepower for flight performance. In March, some UK-based BGs began to remove the chin turret from some of

Below: Not all B-17 missions were in anger. Here, 94th BG B-17Gs fly "low and slow", dropping an array of parachute-retarded supply canisters to Allied troops.

their aircraft, the ball turret from others, and in some cases both. Aircraft speed was improved by up to 25mph (40km) as a result.

VICTORY

On 31 March, the legendary Luftwaffe fighter ace Adolf Galland moved to München-Riem with the last of Germany's newly-formed Me 262 units, the elite Jagdverband 44 (JV: Fighter Formation 44). At times forced to operate from temporary airstrips such as the Munich-Augsburg autobahn, it claimed around 50 "kills" before being overrun on 3 May.

In its last days, there were no 8th AF B-17s for the Luftwaffe jets to hunt. The *"Mighty Eighth"* had flown its last combat mission on 25 April, a strike against the Skoda works at Pilsen. Since its first mission to Rouen, France, in August 1942, the 8th AF had dropped 696,450 tons (705,561 tonnes) of bombs. There were literally no military targets left worth the effort of mounting a B-17 attack. For the Flying Fortress and her crews — around 2,300 aircraft equipping 106 squadrons in the UK, and 500 with 24 squadrons in Italy — the war was effectively over.

The Seattle production line had delivered its last B-17G on 13 April, and was now closed. Next to close was the Douglas line which had built 2,395, followed by Lockheed Vega. On 29 July, aircraft 44-85841 — Vega's 2,250th and final B-17G — passed its post-assembly inspection. The B-17 production run had ended.

Almost a decade had passed since the first flight of the Boeing Model 299. Although the B-17 served at the same time as aircraft such as the Avro Lancaster, it represented an earlier generation of technology. By the middle years of the war its contemporaries were obsolete, yet the Flying Fortress was forced to soldier on.

The USAAF effectively jumped a generation of bombers, passing from the B-17 to the ambitious B-29 Superfortress. The B-17 was not the ideal weapon with which to fight in 1943 and 1944. Despite that, the loss rate it experienced was not markedly different from that of the RAF's night bombers. The skies over Germany were a dangerous place, by day or by night. The B-17 may not have been the best bomber of the era, but like the men who flew her, she accomplished the job she was given.

Perhaps the last word on the B-17

Below: With the end of the war, life began to return to normal around the airfields of rural England. For the B-17s now at rest, there would be just one more flight — back to the USA.

Right: Two generations of bomber from the Boeing stable, with a B-17 leading the way for the aircraft that dropped the atom bomb: the B-29 Superfortress.

Flying Fortress operations during the Second World War should be left to one of her former enemies. In the late-1960s, the author showed an air-to-air photograph of a battle-damaged B-24 Liberator to a former Bf 109G fighter pilot. Was it possible that an aircraft with so little apparent damage could have fallen from the sky within a few seconds of the photo being taken, as the accompanying caption suggested? The former pilot recognized the B-24 immediately. "Those ones were easy to shoot down," he explained. "One good burst of gunfire into a Liberator, and down it would go,

particularly if hit in the wing. Not like that damned Flying Fortress, which just kept on flying . . ."

THE end of the war in Europe sounded the death-knell for the huge B-17 force, with the vast majority being flown back to the United States to languish in several "boneyards" before being declared surplus to requirements and broken up. But the final chapter in the story of the B-17 — its post-war service — had yet to be written.

Such was the pace of combat operations during the war that many B-17s were retired as "War Weary" — unfit for further combat use. A common fate for these retired Fortresses was to be stripped of their armour and armament, and used as makeshift transports. Over 50 such "hacks" were used by the 8th AF alone, with the survivors carrying on such work through the late-1940s and early-1950s as CB-17s. Conditions in the cabin were rather primitive; but the same cannot be said of the VB-17G. As its designation suggests, this model was used as a VIP transport, serving until the mid-1950s.

In addition, two B-17Es and two B-17Fs were converted for evaluation as transports. With all armament bar its nose and tail guns removed, the first of the two Es had extra side windows and seating for up to 38 passengers added. Redesignated XC-108, the aircraft was christened

Above: In service with the 10th Rescue Squadron, USAF during the 1950s, this SB-17G displays both the chin-mounted radar housing and the large, air-delivered lifeboat.

"Bataan" and used by General Douglas MacArthur as his personal airborne transport.

The second of the Es became the sole XC-108A, and was fitted with an outsize cargo door in the port fuselage to facilitate the loading of cargo. All of its armament was deleted. Similarly, the two Fs were completely disarmed; the first one became the YC-108

Below: Possibly the most famous B-17 modified for transport work was the XC-108 named "Bataan", used by General MacArthur as his personal transport.

Above: Weighing in at 3,500lb (1,590kg), and measuring just over 27ft (8.24m) in length, the lifeboat's descent to the water was parachute-retarded.

executive transport, while the second aircraft became the XC-108B aerial fuel tanker.

Three of the post-war B-17 variants were used in the maritime role. The B-17H search and rescue (SAR) model was created in 1945 by fitting 50 B-17Gs with a chin-mounted sea-search radar and a large, droppable lifeboat. Armament was gradually deleted in an attempt to save weight and thus increase the aircraft's effective range. However, machine-guns were soon sprouting from the airframe once again when the aircraft (by now designated SB-17G) were called upon

to fly dangerously close to enemy territory during the Korean War. In addition to serving with the USAF's Air Rescue Service, a dozen SB-17Gs were supplied to the Brazilian Air Force in the early-1950s.

In 1945, the US Navy acquired a single B-17F and no less than 30 ex-USAAF B-17Gs. Fitted with APS-20 sea-search radar housed in a ventral radome, these unarmed aircraft were known as PB-1Ws and were used in the anti-submarine warfare (ASW) role for several years.

The third maritime operator of the Flying Fortress was the United States Coast Guard (USCG), with 17 examples known as PB-1Gs being acquired. These were in fact B-17Gs brought up to SB-17G standard for use in the SAR and aerial-mapping roles. The final PB-1G was retired in 1959.

Not so long-lived were the many surplus B-17s assigned to support US post-war guided missile research programmes. The fortunate ones were used as launch platforms for first-generation guided weapons such as the *Razon* bomb and the JB-2 copy of Germany's wartime V-1 "flying bomb". The vast majority, however, were used as little more than aerial targets during a large number of post-war missile test firings.

Below: Although a small number of the US Navy's PB-1Ws carried the APS-20 radar atop the forward fuselage, most aircraft carried it in a ventral radome.

Above: Despite its camouflage and machine-guns, the sole B-17G to serve with the Dominican Air Force was primarily used to carry out transport duties.

Equipped with TV transmitters and radio-control equipment, these QB-17L/Ps were "flown" by Fortresses variously designated CQ-4, DB-17G/P and QB-17P, all of which acted as drone directors in a similar fashion to those aircraft used in the *Aphrodite* and *Castor* programmes during the Second World War. Needless to say, the fleet of QB-17s steadily diminished as a result of these distinctly "one-way" missions, and all had been expended by June 1960. Unmanned B-17s were also used as instrumented trials aircraft in 1946 as part of the US nuclear test programme.

LIMITED EXPORTS

While such specialized roles provided a further lease of life for the Flying Fortress, there was little call for it to be used in its original bomber role during the post-war years. A few examples did serve briefly with the air forces of countries such as Bolivia, Denmark, the Dominican Republic, France and Portugal, but mostly as transports rather than bombers.

One nation which did see the B-17 as a useful long-range bomber in the late-1940s was Israel. In June 1948, less than a month after declaring its independence, the fledgling Jewish state successfully smuggled three ex-USAAF B-17Gs from the United States to Czechoslovakia via Panama and Portugal. A fourth example was intercepted en route and was forced to abort its flight.

POST-WAR MODELS	
CB-17G	Transport
CQ-4	Drone Director
DB-17G	Drone Director
DB17P	Drone Director
EB-17G	Engine Testbed
FB-17F	Reconnaissance
FB-17G	Reconnaissance
JB-17G	Engine Testbed
MB-17G	Target Drone
PB-1	Testing
PB-1G	Air-Sea Rescue
PB-1W	Maritime Patrol
QB-17G	Target Drone
QB-17L	Target Drone
QB-17N	Target Drone
QB-17P	Target Drone
RB-17F	Reconnaissance
RB-17G	Reconnaissance
SB-17G	Air-Sea Rescue
TB-17G	Pilot Training
VB-17G	Transport
XB-17F	Testing
XB-17G	Testing
XPB-1W	Engine Testbed
ZB-17F	Miscellaneous

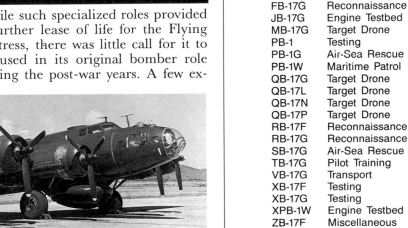

Soldiering On

Their Eastern European destination may seem odd, but the Czechs had been supplying Israel with military equipment since January 1948, and had made an airfield at Zatec available. This was the temporary home for the trio of bombers, all of which eventually arrived there in the final week of June. All three were then fitted with Czech-built Skoda machine-guns, then serviced to prepare them for the onward flight to Israel.

Above: In a typically audacious move, Israel "acquired" three ex-USAAF B-17s, and promptly used them to bomb Arab targets while on their delivery flight.

Below: Suitably devoid of nearly all markings, this all-black RB-17G was used on clandestine agent-dropping missions over North Vietnam during the 1950s.

Above: The old and the new sit together on the Boeing apron, with the veteran SB-17G all but dwarfed by the shape of things to come — the eight-engined, all-jet YB-52 Stratofortress.

Early on the morning of 15 July, the aircraft lumbered into the air and headed south over Austria. They were heavy with fuel — and 500lb (227kg) bombs. This was not going to be a regular delivery flight! Flying down the Adriatic Coast, then east across the Aegean Sea, the trio made a final rendezvous over the island of Crete before heading for individual Arab targets, including Cairo International Airport in Egypt. All targets were successfully bombed, and the aircraft landed in Israel late that night.

A ceasefire three days later brought the conflict to a temporary halt, leaving Egyptian forces still in control of some parts of the Negev Desert. But the B-17s were to be used again in late-1948, this time in conjunction with modified Douglas C-47 Skytrains and Curtiss C-46 Commandos, on nocturnal bombing missions. Further B-17 missions were flown by day, and an official history of the Israel Defence Force/Air Force (IDF/AF) contains a high-altitude photograph showing bombs landing on targets in the Rafa area on the Gaza Strip.

FINAL COMBAT

The subsequent combat career of the Flying Fortress with the IDF/AF is almost undocumented. They may have been used again that winter in another campaign which drove the Egyptian forces from their last positions in the Negev Desert. Whatever the answers, the B-17's usefulness was soon eclipsed by the smaller and much faster de Havilland Mosquito fighter-bomber, more than 200 of which were acquired by Israel in the early-1950s. Nevertheless, two of the veteran four-engined bombers soldiered on and were still in service during the Sinai Campaign of 1956.

Various transport conversions were carried out in the United States during the 1940s and 1950s, although

Above: Radically modified for use by Pratt & Whitney as an engine test-bed, this JB-17G demonstrates to good effect the power of the XT34-P experimental engine.

Above: A handful of B-17s traded explosives for fire-retardant as they took on the role of forest fire-fighters. This example was being used as late as 1985.

civilian use of these B-17s was primarly a South American affair. Cheap to purchase, and more than capable of operating in the "hot and high" environments, civilian B-17 transports were still serving with airlines such as Lloyd Aero Boliviano as recently as the early-1980s.

Possibly the most radically modified Flying Fortresses were a pair of EB-17G (later JB-17G) engine testbeds, operated by Curtiss-Wright and Pratt & Whitney. Easily the most recognizable of modified B-17s, both aircraft had their cockpits moved aft and sported new noses fitted to house test engines. Curtiss-Wright initially used their EB-17G to test the XT35-W turboprop engine during 1947-48. The aircraft subsequently flew with an XT64-GE in place, and later with an XJ65-W powerplant located in an undernose position. Pratt & Whitney used their aircraft to test the XT34-P engine in the early-1950s.

Worthy of mention as possibly the most spectacular and dangerous work carried out by civilian B-17s is the role of firebomber. As with several other large, multi-engined aircraft, the B-17 was pressed into service in the United

States to douse the huge forest fires that erupt every year. At lcast five B-17s were converted for such tasks, their bomb bay doors being opened and a sheet of water or chemical fire suppressant released as the aircraft passed low over a fire.

Sadly, such operations are now a thing of the past. The passage of time

and an inevitable lack of spares gradually forced these veterans into retirement, some 50 years after the first of the breed took to the air. Thankfully, the Flying Fortress lives on, cared for and flown by aviation enthusiasts interested in preserving what many regard as the classic long-range bomber of all time.

Below: One of a small number of B-17s still flying, "Shoo Shoo BABY" is also the only survivor to have been used in combat during the Second World War.

INDEX